The Cross-Cultural Parenting Playbook

Full details of all our other publications can be found on http://www.multilingual-matters.com, or by writing to Multilingual Matters, BLOCK, The Fairfax, Pithay Ct, Bristol, BS1 3BN, UK.

The Cross-Cultural Parenting Playbook

Sangita Shresthova

MULTILINGUAL MATTERS
Bristol • Jackson

DOI https://doi.org/10.21832/SHREST1367
Library of Congress Cataloging in Publication Data
A catalog record for this book is available from the Library of Congress.
Library of Congress Control Number (LCCN): 2025032221.
British Library Cataloguing in Publication Data
A catalogue entry for this book is available from the British Library.

ISBN-13: 978-1-78892-136-7 (hbk)
ISBN-13: 978-1-78892-135-0 (pbk)

Multilingual Matters
UK: BLOCK, The Fairfax, Pithay Ct, Bristol, BS1 3BN, UK.
USA: Ingram, Jackson, TN, USA.
Authorised Representative: Easy Access System Europe – Mustamäe tee 50, 10621
Tallinn, Estonia, gpsr.requests@easproject.com.

Website: https://www.multilingual-matters.com
X: Multi_Ling_Mat
Bluesky: @multi-ling-mat.bsky.social
Facebook: https://www.facebook.com/multilingualmatters
Blog: https://www.channelviewpublications.wordpress.com

The policy of Multilingual Matters/Channel View Publications is to use papers that
are natural, renewable and recyclable products, made from wood grown in sustainable
forests. In the manufacturing process of our books, and to further support our policy,
preference is given to printers that have FSC and PEFC Chain of Custody certification.
The FSC and/or PEFC logos will appear on those books where full certification has
been granted to the printer concerned.

Typeset by Riverside Publishing Solutions.

Contents

Prologue

My name is Marek and I am in 5th grade.
My name is Marek and I'm Czech,
With Czech grandparents and a Czech class grade,
With Czech relatives who I know by name.
My name is Marek and I am Nepali
I love the momos our family friends make,
The curries, the meats, the vegetables with rice.
My name is Marek and I am Indian,
The poojas, the colors, the dosas are great.
My name is Marek and I am American,
I like giving high fives and the ten lane freeways.
My name is Marek and when you look at me
You might not see much of the cultures that are mixed.
But when I start talking, what's hidden comes out.
Then you can see who really is 'me'.
So when I watch other people, I like to think:
'Who really are these people all the way in?'
What cultures, interests, and ideas do they keep within?
I like to find out, to ask them and see,
And that way they can also learn about me.

Written by Marek D. (age 10)
This is a poem I wrote reflecting on
my mom writing this book.

Part 1
Understand Cross-Cultural Identities and Parenting

1   Where the Story Begins

A man, a woman and a small child hurtle through Kathmandu's foggy streets on a small Honda motorcycle. The man and woman in this story are my parents. My mom is Czech, my father Nepali. I am the child sandwiched between them. We take a sharp right and park in front of the Nepal Telecommunications office. We enter the empty hall and crowd into a phone booth to place our annual phone call to wish relatives in (then) Czechoslovakia a happy new year. The call connects and my grandmother picks up, her voice slightly distorted. I struggle to find words and hold back tears. Her voice seems familiar but distant, coming to me from a different reality somewhere far away. I clutch the phone receiver tightly and immediately forget what I had wanted to tell her. Then a resolute click ends our 180 seconds of prepaid contact. I feel like a door has just slammed shut, leaving me feeling hollow and unfulfilled. I will not speak with my grandmother again until months later, relying on Nepal's unpredictable postal system to deliver letters in the meantime.

Fast forward many years (more than I care to admit), I sit at our dining table in Los Angeles, California, and watch my 10-year-old son casually tap my iPhone to initiate a FaceTime call with his grandmother (my mother) in the Czech Republic. She picks up; her voice clear and strong and waves to him happily. She is not in the least surprised that her grandson, Marek, has called. They share what's new and then decide to play a quick game of Czech Wordle. Marek shares his screen, and they mull over what the word of the day might be. As I watch them, I am struck by just how different my son's experience of growing up across cultures has been from the one I had. I had a three-minute call. He has a daily FaceTime and so much more.

Cross-Cultural Parenting in a Connected World

It goes without saying that Marek is growing up in a world far more interconnected than the one I knew as a child living in Nepal. My younger years were defined by international calls, phone cards, dial-up and later Skype, CDs, VCDs and DVDs. His daily interactions with family and cultures across the globe tap WhatsApp, streaming video, and podcasts, reflecting the possibilities of a connected world that I barely even dreamed of as a child. It's a poignant reminder of how far we've come, and yet it also raises new questions about how to foster meaningful cultural connections for children growing up in a confusing and challenging media-filled world. How can we ensure that these connections are deep rather than superficial and fleeting? And more broadly, what role can we as parents play in guiding children to engage critically and thoughtfully with the cultural influences they encounter?

As a child of a Czechoslovakian mother and Nepali father who moved between countries, I have first-hand experience of what it means to grow up between cultures. For years, I made it a point to call many cities home from Kathmandu to Prague, via London, Berlin, Los Angeles, and others. For a long time, I was happiest when my bags were packed and ready to go, living in transit between places, finding roots in communities not geographies. As a media researcher who specializes in youth and digital media, I've spent much of my professional life exploring how media shapes our understanding of identity and belonging across cultural boundaries. As a professor at the University of Southern California, I focus on how people and communities use media for social impact.

And yet, becoming a parent and raising Marek as a multilingual Czech-Nepali Indian-American has made these themes even more urgent. From enrolling him in weekly Czech language classes online to listening to Bollywood songs that connect him to his South Asian heritage, I now know both the joys and pitfalls of raising a cross-cultural child. And there are so many more questions. When and how should I introduce my son to different cultures, and how can I make these exposures meaningful? What's the value in exposing him to so many cultures? Won't he just be confused by it all? How can media help, and how much should I take on board all the concerns that have been raised about youth and social media? Where can I find a community to support me in this journey? And, how do I accept that his cross-cultural experience will be so different from mine?

These questions have kept me up at night, making me realize just how deeply this matters to me. Cross-cultural parenting wasn't just a passing curiosity or an abstract concept. It is a profound passion, one that has shaped not only how I see my role as a parent but also how I understand my own identity as I move through this world. This is a really big deal, at least to me.

Stories from Cross-Cultural Families

To understand how others parent across cultures, I first turned to friends, family and online parent communities to learn about people's experiences. Soon, cross-cultural parenting started to come up in many conversations I was having. A friend shared that she takes her children on virtual YouTube tours of her home village they have actually never visited. A colleague laughingly explained that he and his partner had conversations about how they were going to use media to bridge between his Mexican and her European heritage even before their child was born. I started to gather these stories, noticing that they are both unique to each family's circumstance and similar in their continued negotiation around priorities that parents set, possibilities they identify and limitations they face.

Overwhelmingly, the stories these parents shared soon confirmed that media (broadly defined) plays a huge role in many parents' efforts to raise their children across cultures. These seemingly small actions can serve as cultural lifelines, each media choice an intentional attempt to connect children to their roots. Parents create playlists of songs from their childhoods. They include lullabies in almost forgotten languages, old Bollywood hits or folk songs from remote villages. These then become material to share during bedtime routines or family gatherings. Some parents cook alongside YouTube chefs, learning and teaching traditional recipes that might have been lost across generations. Suitcases filled with books, carefully selected from far-off bookstores or family libraries, represent more than reading material; they carry stories, histories, and cultural values. WhatsApp calls become a space where children learn family jokes, overhear elders telling stories and practice their heritage languages in real-time conversations. For these parents, media isn't just about consumption. It is an essential, everyday tool for building bridges across languages, time zones and identities.

Over the next few months, my project grew.

In the end, I interviewed over 30 parents and caregivers (and some young people) from diverse countries and communities who see themselves as bridging cultures. The families I met reflected a broad spectrum of backgrounds, including parents who see themselves bridging Afghan, Iraqi, Czech, South Korean, Indian, Nepali, American, Dutch, Montenegrin, Nigerian, Argentinian and Costa Rican, American cultures, among others. These families' experiences spanned continents and cultures, from Hindu traditions to Chinese diasporic practices.

I also fielded a survey with 94 parents and caregivers through international schools, as well as bilingual and multicultural parenting groups. The responses I received reflect the breadth of the participants' affiliations, with some identifying as mixed-race or third-culture kids (TCKs), and others representing specific national, ethnic and linguistic identities such as Armenian, African-American, Puerto Rican, Egyptian, Australian, British, Colombian, Finnish, Latin-American, South African, Jewish, Germanic, Southeast Asian and Slavic. Many parents also brought religious affiliations (including Muslim, Christian and non-religious perspectives) into their parenting approaches. To be clear most, though not all, of the parents I interviewed reside in the United States or Europe.

I also spent hundreds of hours in parenting groups on social media, where I encountered stories about the day-to-day realities of cross-cultural families. Many of these groups are dedicated to parents supporting multiple languages in their homes, offering advice on everything from choosing the right bilingual books to navigating language preferences with extended family members. To parents committed to cross-cultural parenting, these platforms become spaces for exchanging tips on how to nurture fluency in heritage languages, commiserating over the challenges of language loss, and celebrating when a child uses a new word in their second or third language. These groups also provide support for navigating the broader complexities of cross-cultural parenting, such as balancing cultural traditions or figuring out how to celebrate multiple holidays.

Along the way, I made it a point to sign up for groups aimed at supporting parents as they navigate their own cross-cultural identities. For example, one Facebook group I participated in was run by psychologists and focused on providing peer support to Czechs (mostly women) contemplating a 'return' to their country of origin after spending years, sometimes decades, abroad. These discussions highlighted layered and often emotional questions of belonging, reintegration and identity for both parents and children. In spaces like this, I found parents grappling with the challenge of bridging their personal and cultural histories while also striving to give their children a sense of rootedness in a dynamic, global world. These groups revealed not just the practicalities of cross-cultural parenting, but also the emotional work involved in navigating the evolving identities of both parents and their families.

And, I got involved in schools and programs focused on supporting heritage languages and cultural traditions. I enrolled my son in the Czech School in Los Angeles, which is a Saturday program dedicated to teaching the Czech language and celebrating Czech culture. He also attended Petite Library, an afterschool program in Altadena, California, that immersed children in French language and cultural experiences. Through these programs, I not only observed but connected with other parents raising bilingual and bicultural children. These experiences gave me first-hand insight into how community-led initiatives can create a sense of belonging and continuity for families.

All of these conversations, encounters and experiences shaped my understanding of cross-cultural parenting and deeply informed what I share with you here.

The Growing Understanding of Cross-Cultural Parenting

To me, this book is not just a collection of individual stories but also a reflection of what I see as a growing understanding of what it means to parent across cultures. This understanding places cross-cultural parenting at the center, rather than the margins, of what families of today experience. Far from being a niche concern, cross-cultural parenting reflects broader societal shifts toward interconnectedness and bridging of divides. As I listened to stories from parents navigating everything from heritage language retention to cultural identity formation, I began to see how their experiences embodied critical themes of the current moment.

Every day, every month, every year, the number of cross-cultural, interracial and mixed families, households, parents and children grows, reflecting a global shift toward increased cultural diversity within families. According to recent data from the International Organization for Migration, the number of international migrants worldwide has reached 281 million, marking a significant increase over the past two decades and resulting in more families formed across nationalities and cultures.[1] In the United States, interracial marriage has grown markedly over the past several decades. Approximately 19% of newlyweds were married to someone of a different race or ethnicity in 2019, a significant rise from just 3% in 1967.[2] This trend reflects broader societal changes and increasing acceptance of diverse family structures as the 2020 US Census showed significant growth in people (especially young people) identifying as multiracial.[3] Similarly, in Europe, around 1 in 12 marriages involves a native-born and a foreign-born spouse, illustrating the region's growing cross-cultural demographic.[4]

While statistics are harder to find, the trend of cross-cultural and international marriages is not limited to Europe and the United States but is also evident in other regions around the globe. In South Korea, for instance, marriages involving foreign-born spouses peaked at 13.5% in 2005 and remain a consistent feature of the country's demographic landscape, contributing to its growing multiculturalism[5]. Similarly, Taiwan saw international marriages account for 32% of all unions in 2003 before stabilizing at 13% in the following decade due to policy changes.[6] In China, international marriages have been shaped by the presence of foreign students, with individuals from regions such as Africa, South Asia and the Middle East forming families during their studies.[7]

This increase in cross-cultural families reflects broader migratory patterns driven by various factors: refugees fleeing conflict, economic migrants seeking opportunities, missionaries and international professionals relocating for work and individuals moving for love and forming families in cross-cultural marriages.[8] In this sense, our world has become more interconnected making it ever more important for us to understand and support families navigating these diverse cultural identities.

Situating this Book

In writing this book, I turned first to the wealth of literature on cross-cultural parenting and the experiences of families living in multiple worlds. To be clear, there is a rich body of work that sheds light on these topics from various angles, offering deep insights and practical guidance. Seminal works like *Third Culture Kids* by David C. Pollock and Ruth E. Van Reken provided a foundational understanding of the emotional and social complexities faced by children raised in multicultural environments.[9] Their concept of the 'Third Culture Kid' (TCK), a child raised in a culture different from their parents, has become a cornerstone in discussions about identity, belonging and the long-term effects of growing up across cultures.

Other works, such as Casey E. Bales' *Invisible Outsider* and Marilyn R. Gardner's *Worlds Apart,* take a more personal approach, recounting the authors' own stories of growing up amid frequent relocations.[10] These narratives capture the paradox of this lifestyle: the struggles of being an outsider everywhere but also the unique comfort that comes with living in-between. Similarly, Farzana Nayani's *Raising Multiracial Children* explores the challenges of parents and children whose identities span multiple racial or cultural backgrounds.[11] Nayani offers practical strategies for navigating conversations about race and identity, equipping parents with tools to help their children embrace their multifaceted heritage.

Academic research further enriches the understanding of cross-cultural parenting. Marc H. Bornstein and others' work on cultural approaches to parenting underscores how deeply parenting practices are influenced by cultural values and norms, while Bahira Sherif Trask's *Globalization and Families* examines how global interconnectedness reshapes family dynamics.[12] Comparative studies, such as *Families Across Cultures: A 30-Nation Psychological Study* edited by James Georgas and colleagues, highlight both universal patterns and culture-specific differences in family structures.[13] Similarly, *Cross-Cultural Family Research and Practice* by W. Kim Halford and Fons Van de Vijver bridges theory and application, offering insights into how families adapt to cultural transitions.[14] Broader reviews, like those found in Amanda Morris and Jennifer Lansford's contribution to *The Cambridge Handbook of Parenting*, offer invaluable resources for understanding the broader societal trends shaping cross-cultural parenting.[15]

These and other existing works have been instrumental in providing context and inspiration for my own journey. I also noticed a distinct gap that I aim to fill with this book. While much of the literature focuses on broad trends, personal journeys or theoretical frameworks, my book offers a unique perspective: the lived, everyday experiences of cross-cultural parents from a wide range of cultural, geographic and economic contexts. In this book, economic migrants in Los Angeles balance their children's integration into a new society with preserving connections to their homeland. Nepali expats navigate the dissonance of raising children abroad while preparing them for a 'home' that may feel foreign.

In Kentucky, newly arrived Afghan families face the immense challenge of building a life in a country that offers no possibility of return. In contrast, serial expat families move across borders by choice, focusing less on survival and more on fostering their children's evolving identities and sense of belonging. By focusing on the practical and tangible aspects of parenting across cultures, this book brings the abstract challenges of cross-cultural parenting into the realm of the relatable, actionable and real.

Media is Unavoidable

There is one more thing that makes this book different, namely my recognition that old AND new media and popular culture are central to the lives of many cross-cultural families. Whether it is Afghan parents using WhatsApp to maintain contact with family members left behind, or expat parents streaming content from multiple countries to connect their children with diverse cultures, media plays an indispensable role in bridging distances, maintaining languages and fostering a sense of continuity in an otherwise fragmented existence.

This reality coexists with a cautionary development marked by an ever-growing number of books and studies that discuss the impact of media on children's development, highlighting the need for balanced screen time and the importance of age-appropriate content. And yes, there are real and legitimate reasons to be concerned about the role of some media in our daily lives. We should be worried about online privacy. We should be worried about the psychological impact of constantly comparing oneself to others as researchers like Jonathan Haidt draw our attention to the correlation between increased social media use and rising rates of anxiety and depression in young people.[16] Other studies have shown how algorithms can amplify harmful content, from disinformation to dangerous body image ideals, leaving parents feeling like they must constantly be vigilant. Indeed, we should be worried about disinformation and pornography and how these materials can find their way into the lives of young, impressionable people.

So, many parents, including me, are concerned about navigating 'screen time' management, online safety and cyberbullying. Books like *iGen* by Jean M. Twenge underscore the generational shift in how children and teens interact with media, highlighting the challenges and implications of growing up in a digital age.[17] These perspectives are valuable in highlighting the risks and challenges that come with a media-saturated world. At the same time, all the parents I met acknowledge that media is here to stay and will inevitably be a part of our family lives. The challenge, then, is not whether to embrace media but how to do so intentionally, ensuring that it becomes a tool for connection and growth rather than a source of harm.

Parenting by Any Media

That is why I take a broader, more expansive, approach to media and popular culture and put us as parents in the 'driver's seat' as we navigate our media-saturated world. I specifically focus on children under the age of 12 and stress that media can lead to shared intergenerational experiences for this age group.

As a media researcher, I think about media both broadly and specifically. I use the term 'media' to refer to a wide range of communication technologies and the social behaviors that grow up around them. I include new media technologies and older analog options. This means I look at books AND tablets. I consider live dance and user-generated videos. In other words, I look at all the media that surrounds us in our daily lives.

I use the term 'popular culture' to refer not only to media content but also to the meaningful relationships we share with each other around that content. Popular culture refers to the sum total of everyday human experiences, how we think and live, the stories we tell, the media content we seek out and the things we do. And popular culture is not simply something we passively consume; it is also something we actively *create* and *do*.

The parents I met *create* and *do* a lot. They join groups on social media to get their hands on hard-to-find foreign-language children's books. They organize music nights in their homes to perform live renditions of the songs on their Spotify lists for their family and friends. They enroll their kids in online language courses and download international educational apps. From streaming documentaries, to mailing books across countries, from online cooking tutorials to shopping at the neighborhood international foods shop, these parents are finding creative approaches to making a cross-cultural upbringing meaningful, engaging and connected. I would say they are parenting *by any media* (more on this in Chapter 4).

Raising Cross-Cultural Kids Matters

Despite their different backgrounds and life circumstances, the parents I met agreed on one thing: raising cross-cultural kids is worth the effort. Cross-cultural parenting nurtures children's understanding of shared family values and provides them with a deep sense of where they came from. It connects them to different parts of the world, fostering an appreciation and sensitivity towards other people and cultures. Eventually, this multicultural upbringing enables children to adapt more easily and choose where they want to live, encouraging them to develop a sense of global awareness. My survey data reveals that nearly all respondents find it crucial for their children to grow up experiencing more than one culture. Over 90% of participants indicate that raising children with multiple cultural influences fosters global awareness and encourages sensitivity to other people and traditions. Parents emphasize the importance of helping children understand their heritage, with 83% highlighting the value of connecting them to their roots. These efforts are seen as integral to equipping children with the skills needed to navigate an increasingly interconnected world, with 72% of respondents noting that cross-cultural exposure helps children develop important future skills. In other words, the parents I surveyed believe that cross-cultural parenting helps their children acquire valuable skills that will benefit them in the future.

By growing up in an environment where diverse cultural norms and practices are part of daily life, children learn to navigate change with ease and approach problems with a flexible mindset. This ability to understand and integrate different viewpoints equips them to handle the complexities and uncertainties of our global society, fostering resilience and innovation. In short, cross-cultural parenting sets up children to embrace their shifting and evolving identity.

Of course, the parents and I acknowledge that raising children across different cultures can also be hard. Finding time to engage in cultural activities regularly can be challenging, and the financial cost of purchasing books, films and other materials or traveling to maintain cultural connections can be substantial. Travel restrictions can add an additional burden and separate families. Cross-cultural parents can sometimes feel isolated, and children may be different from their peers. It can be challenging for cross-cultural families to feel connected to a local community, and finding suitable materials to use can be hard. This can make it difficult for the family to feel rooted in a particular place, adding another layer of complexity to the parenting journey. Despite these challenges, the parents I met believe the benefits of a multicultural upbringing outweigh the difficulties, fostering a deep sense of identity and global awareness in their children.

About this Book

All in all, I want this book to be a personable, practical introduction to cross-cultural parenting. I draw on my own experience, research, and stories from families of diverse backgrounds. Each chapter reflects a specific aspect of the journey, offering insights, strategies, and activities. I wrote this book with the understanding that some of you will want to read the book cover to cover. Others will want to skip the sections that interest you most. So, here is the road-map:

Part 1: Understanding Cross-Cultural Identities and Parenting

(1) Chapter 1 – Where the Story Begins

In this opening chapter (which you just read), I reflected on my journey as a cross-cultural parent and why it inspired me to write this book. Through personal stories and insights from other families, I explored the challenges and rewards of raising children across cultures. I explained why this work matters and how it connects to our global, interconnected world.

(2) Chapter 2 – Embrace In-Between

Here, I discuss the importance of getting alignment between parents, caregivers and relatives within families when it comes to cultural priorities. Stories from families highlight how negotiating values upfront helps create cohesive approaches to parenting across cultures.

(3) Chapter 3 – Get on the Same Page

In this chapter I explore the complexities of belonging for those of us living in two (or more) cultures. Parents share how they navigate homesickness, identity formation and finding comfort in occupying that space in-between.

Part 2: Bridge with Media and Popular Culture

(4) Chapter 4 – By Any Media

Old and new media play a central role in maintaining cultural ties. In this chapter, I explore how parents use tools like WhatsApp, YouTube, and streaming platforms to foster connections. Whether through bedtime stories or video calls, media can help parents bridge geographical and cultural divides.

(5) Chapter 5 – Connect Through Pop Culture

Pop culture offers opportunities for playful cultural engagement. In this chapter we peek into how families use movies, music and books to inspire conversations, compare cultural stories and build shared narratives across generations.

Part 3: Cross Cultures in Everyday Life

(6) Chapter 6 – Feed the Imagination

Food connects people across cultures, and in this chapter, I explore how families bond over cooking and experimenting with traditional recipes. Parents describe how culinary practices convey cultural stories and pique their children's curiosity.

(7) Chapter 7 – Sing and Dance

Music and dance can offer joyful ways to engage with heritage. I share how participating in cultural dance classes, learning dance moves through YouTube and downloading traditional songs offers opportunities for physically experienced cultural moments.

(8) Chapter 8 – Play With Languages

Multilingualism is a gateway to different cultures. I explore how parents encourage playful language learning at home, creating a media-assisted environment where children naturally switch between languages and blend linguistic influences.

Part 4: Build and Sustain Connection Across Distance

(9) Chapter 9 – Seek Out Communities

In this chapter I highlight the importance of finding in-person and virtual communities. Through potlucks, language classes, discussion boards and cultural festivals, families discover support networks that make cross-cultural parenting more sustainable and joyful.

(10) Chapter 10 – Visit and Connect, Even Virtually

Travel may not always be possible, but virtual connections offer rich ways to engage with family and cultural heritage. I am honest about the emotional realities of long-distance family relationships and how media can offer meaningful connections despite the miles.

Part 5: Navigate the Paths Ahead

(11) Chapter 11 – Accept the Journey

I conclude that there really is no single way to parent cross-cultures. Parenting is a fluid and evolving journey. Sometimes it's smooth, sometimes challenging. I invite you to embrace the process and recognize that every effort you make opens doors for your children.

To connect the themes discussed with your own lives (dear readers), I end each chapter with reflective questions. These questions encourage you to consider your own experiences, beliefs and practices, fostering a deeper understanding of how you can apply the insights from the chapter to your parenting journey.

I also include a brief, playful prompt or activity that you can explore with your children. Inspired by the experiences of the parents I met over the course of researching this book, these activities are designed to engage families with the key themes in a hands-on, enjoyable way. For example, a chapter on the importance of music and dance in cultural expression might suggest creating a family playlist of songs from different cultures and having a freestyle dance party at home.

Who is this Book For?

This book is for anyone raising or caring for children across cultures and wondering how to make those connections meaningful. As someone who grew up bridging Nepali and Czech cultures, and who now raises my son across Czech, Nepali, Indian and American traditions, I understand the joys and pitfalls of navigating this path. Whether you're balancing heritage languages, blending holiday traditions or simply trying to make sense of what it means to raise a child between worlds, this book is here for you.

But this book is also for anyone curious about the complexities of culture and family. Whether you're a teacher working with multicultural classrooms, a grandparent eager to see your heritage reflected in the next generation, or a friend supporting parents who bridge cultures in their homes, this book is for you too.

An Invitation

Whether you are just beginning, feeling stuck or looking back on years of experience in cross-cultural parenting, I hope you find in these pages both practical tools and a sense of connection. As I continue on this journey of raising Marek, I am also learning, experimenting and reflecting. I'm constantly looking for ways to connect him with communities. This might be through local cultural groups or by engaging with supportive parents through social media. Some days, I laugh along with TikTok videos that poke fun at the absurdities of cross-cultural parenting, reminding me that even in our most serious moments, humor can bridge worlds. Other days, I seek out support in a parenting group focused on bilingualism.

So, if there is one lesson that I invite you to take away from this book, it is that there really is no singular, right way to parent across cultures. The process will ebb and flow, shaped by moments of success, moments of confusion and everything in-between. At times, I've struggled with the familiar guilt that I'm not doing enough and feeling overwhelmed by the burden of doing it right. I wonder if I should speak more Czech at home, introduce new holiday traditions, or curate media with greater intention. But I've come to realize that guilt isn't the point.

Whether it's sharing a song from my childhood, reading a bedtime story in a different language or laughing at a cultural joke, each action I take matters.

Whether we or our children ultimately step through that door isn't something we can fully control. And that's okay. The journey of cross-cultural parenting isn't about perfection; it's about showing up, being present, and embracing the richness that comes from trying. Often, the connections we create may unfold in ways we never could have imagined, with our children discovering new meanings, interests and identities that surprise us.

In the end, I just want to extend an invitation to all of you. We have an opportunity to celebrate both where we come from and the possibilities of where we might go.

Notes

(1) International Organization for Migration, 2020.
(2) Geiger & Livingston, 2019.
(3) Rico *et al.*, 2023.
(4) Lanzieri, 2012.
(5) Kim, 2017.
(6) Jones, 2012.
(7) Raja & Tao, 2024.
(8) Catalano, 2016.
(9) Pollock & Van Reken, 2009.
(10) Bales, 2022; Gardner, 2018.
(11) Nayani, 2020.
(12) Bornstein *et al.*, 2011; Trask, 2010.
(13) Georgas, 2006.
(14) Halford & Van de Vijver, 2020.
(15) Morris & Lansford, 2022.
(16) Haidt, 2024.
(17) Twenge, 2017.

Takeaways from Chapter 1

Growing up between cultures opens new worlds. Children with roots in more than one culture learn to see life through a richer, more varied lens that shapes how they understand themselves and others.

Our families tell a bigger story. As cross-cultural households become more common, they reflect the ways our friendships, work and communities stretch across borders.

All the effort pays off. Sure, navigating different traditions and languages can be tough, but parents agree it brings moments of pride, deeper resilience and a genuine sense of belonging.

Parenting is a journey, not a destination. There's no single 'right' way to do this; every choice you make helps your child weave together the different threads of their identity.

Stories and screens can be powerful bridges. Whether it's a favorite commute-time song or a FaceTime call, media gives us tools to keep our children connected to their heritage and the people they love.

2 Embrace In-Between

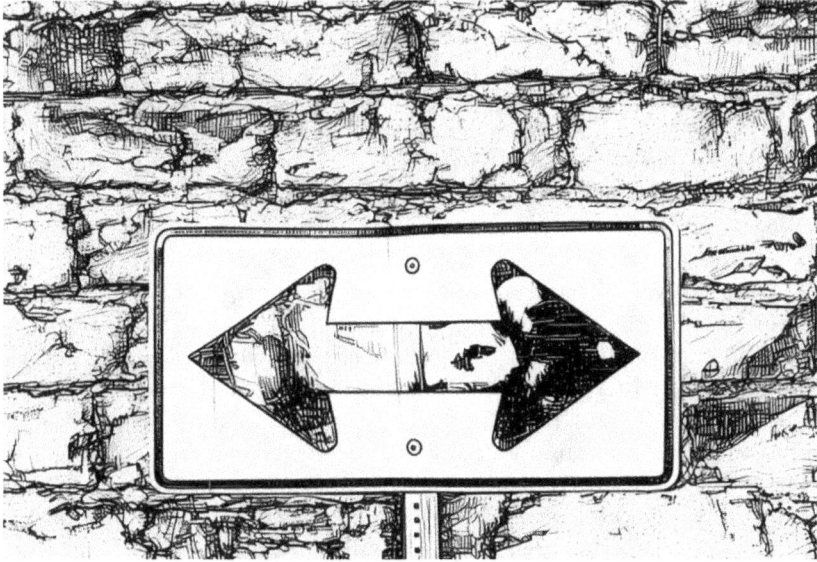

Figure 2.1 Cross-Cultural Identities are complex. (credit: A. Desai)

When Marta was little, she refused to let her identity be reduced to fractions.[1] 'I'm not half Czech and half Chinese', she told her father one day. 'I'm three times something!' In her mind, she was fully Czech, fully Chinese and also Singaporean (the country where she was born). Her father smiled when he shared this anecdote, because he understood the depth of her statement. 'You don't divide yourself', he explained to me. 'You grow'. Marta's claim captures a powerful concept familiar to many with cross-cultural roots. Identity, for us, isn't about splitting between cultures or balancing percentages. It's about layering experiences. It's about multiplying connections. It's about expanding the self. It's the opposite of limiting identity labels and border policing. Like Marta said, we are much more than the sum of our parts.

There is no doubt that living with multiple cultures complicates our sense of home and belonging. Whether we travel or not, we imagine ourselves spanning communities, countries, continents and cultures. We live in-between. Always. I have experienced this firsthand. I know what it means to keep up with multiple time zones in my head and always know what time it is in Kathmandu, Prague and Los Angeles. I sometimes even stop to imagine what it would feel like to walk the streets, see the people, listen to the sounds. As a child, I would close my eyes and imagine I was somewhere else, in another bed, in another city, another country. I have moved around so much that I exist simultaneously in multiple time zones, even as I live in one place.

I share this experience with Sashi, a 26-year-old whose life has also been shaped by moving between countries. Born in Nepal, Sashi's early years involved frequent relocations because of their father's work with an international agency. From the crowded and loud streets of Karachi to the mountainous landscapes of Switzerland, Sashi's sense of self was shaped by international experiences, which informed their worldview and equipped them with the sensitivities to navigate diverse cultural contexts. 'Growing up with multiple cultures, I was always navigating different worlds', Sashi told me when I interviewed them. 'At home, I was Nepali, but out there, I was part of the international community'.

This upbringing gave Sashi a heightened awareness of cultural norms. When they moved from Pakistan to Switzerland, Sashi, then still very small, told their mother, 'Your skirt is too short', showing that they were aware of the more stringent coverage expected of women in Pakistan. And yet, returning to Nepal at age 11 felt alien to Sashi. Though they and their family had been part of Nepali expat communities abroad, their Nepali family labeled them the 'American kid' because of their accent and mannerisms. Over time these challenges actually deepened their understanding of cultural fluidity. Rather than feeling divided, Sashi eventually learned to embrace their in-betweenness.

My own experience has been similar in many ways. Growing up in Nepal, I constantly moved between different cultural spaces. At home, the tone was shaped by my Czech mother. I was encouraged to be direct and pragmatic. With my extended Nepali family my interactions reflected different customs and expectations. I soon learned that I needed to appear respectful when speaking to anyone older than me. At the international school I attended, I needed to appear confident and ready to learn. Over time, I learned how to adapt physically and emotionally to each space. I stood taller and pulled my shoulders back at school, cast my eyes down demurely with my Nepali family and looked my mother directly in the eye at home.

Sashi's story and my own experiences highlight how complex and layered cross-cultural identity can be. Navigating cross-cultural experiences makes us conscious of how we are read by others. These experiences can also teach us to be intentional about what we project and how we adapt to different contexts based on what aspect of our cultural identity we want to share.

Still, making sense of cross-cultural identities can be confusing, which is why we may reach to various frameworks and theories to get clarity on where we come from and how we see our (and our children's) cross-cultural selves. To support this process, I will delve briefly into theoretical approaches such as multiculturalism, integration, biculturalism and the unique experiences of Third Culture Kids to situate how we think about identity in the context of cross-cultural parenting. This overview isn't meant to be exhaustive or academic; it's meant to give us a shared foundation from which to appreciate the possibilities and constraints of these ideas and think through how they might apply to your lives.

Ultimately, I (and others) believe it is a fluid experience of belonging, both here and there, which defines the lives of many cross-cultural kids and adults. Like Marta, cross-cultural kids are more than the sum of their cultural parts.

On Multiculturalism

Decades ago, I was asked to perform a Nepali dance at a Princeton University cultural show. As an international undergraduate student, I was confused by the invitation. On the one hand, this felt like an opportunity to make my background visible to others. On the other hand, the offer also exposed a tension I hadn't fully grappled with before. I had never learned traditional Nepali dancing growing up in Kathmandu. To be honest, I never saw the need for it. And yet, I was now expected to embody and represent this aspect of Nepali culture. I decided to rise to the occasion and quickly came up with some steps and performed them as best as I could to a pre-recorded song.

I thought that would be the end of it, but then a local newspaper published a photo of me with the tagline 'Native of Nepal'. I knew that this label was meant to be a compliment, and yet it made me feel disingenuous or feel like a fraud. Yes, I am partially Nepali, but I am not only Nepali.

To those around me, this was a multicultural moment that I should have celebrated with pride. Instead, it made me acutely aware of how such multicultural approaches force individuals to fit themselves into predefined categories, celebrating diversity in a way that can feel performative or reductive. Looking back at it now, that experience taught me that I needed to learn to be a 'cultural chameleon', that is to say I needed to be versatile, understand the context, and respond accordingly. I also needed to learn to identify cultural expectations and norms and know when to push against them and when to respect them. While useful, the need for these skills also makes the limitations of multiculturalism visible.

In an ironic twist of fate, the whole experience ultimately led me to seek out and learn traditional Nepali dance!

Still, my experience at Princeton echoes the points made by scholars about multiculturalism as it evolved over the past decades. 'First wave' multiculturalism was first and foremost about protecting minority rights in democratic contexts, mostly in the so-called West. Advocates emphasized respect for diverse cultural practices in public spaces like schools, courts, hospitals and government offices.[2] Making accommodations that would allow for these practices was seen as essential to ensuring that minority groups were able to participate fully in broader society. With 'second-wave' multiculturalism, the approach shifted towards sustaining social connections and supporting diversity[3] as scholars explored whether the presence of accommodation policies supported or hindered social cohesion. This question remains central to contemporary debates on multiculturalism.

While helpful in making cultural diversity visible, both of these approaches fail to recognize the nuances of cultural exchange and the ethics of policing cultural boundaries. My experience underscored this failing. I was being celebrated as 'diverse', but to do that I had to perform a culture that was actually not a true reflection of my cross-cultural experiences. This limitation of multiculturalism is even more significant at a time defined by global exchange and transcultural connection, identity mixing and, dare I say, remixing.

Integration, Assimilation and Biculturalism

Multiculturalism is just one way to approach cross-cultural identities in pluralistic societies. Integration, assimilation and biculturalism are additional frameworks we may consider as they shift the focus from institutional accommodations to the lived realities of individuals and communities.

Let me share Aaila's experiences to bring these frameworks to life. When Aaila and her family fled Afghanistan for Kentucky, they were sadly not able to bring any belongings. All they brought with them were their cultural practices and beliefs, their hope for a new beginning, and the fear of what they would lose along the way. When I spoke with her two years after their arrival, Aaila reflected on what they had lived through and what she had learned. 'We are lucky to be here', she told me, 'But it is still hard. We are busy every day working, studying and paying bills, just to stand on our own feet'.

At home, Aaila tries to hold on to the family's Afghan identity. She speaks Farsi with her daughters, cooks traditional meals and mentions stories of their homeland. 'I tell my daughter, "Say it in Farsi"', she shared with me. Aaila also noted that her daughter now mixes English into their conversations. 'She tries, but sometimes she says, "I forgot the word"'. For

Aaila, keeping Afghan culture alive in her home is more than a habit. It is a commitment that grows out of a pressing need for preservation.

Yet, Aaila also wants her daughters to thrive in America and adjust to life in Kentucky. They take music lessons. They are learning to swim. They participate in sports. These are activities Aaila never experienced growing up. 'They are doing this not just for themselves', she explains, 'but for all the girls in Afghanistan who can't even leave their homes now'.

Aaila's story illustrates what we mean by integration, an approach that allows someone to hold on to their cultural identity while they also actively participate in society at large.[4] Her daughters have adapted quickly to their new environment. They are thriving in school. They feel comfortable engaging in extracurricular activities. They also keep up with their Farsi. At first glance, it would appear that they are getting the best of both worlds.

Still, there are limits. Aaila does not share with others in her local Afghan community that her daughters are learning how to swim. She worries about what other Afghan families in the area would think and say. 'If I told them, they would ask, "Why is your daughter doing that?"' she says. Integration can be fraught with tension, especially when cultural context and previously held norms collide.

Assimilation, an approach where one is asked to adopt a dominant culture at the expense of a minority one, asks for even deeper sacrifices.[5] At times, Aaila worries that her daughters' now-American life will eventually pull them away from their Afghan roots. They will form new friendships. They will embrace new technologies. They will develop new expectations of what their future holds. To Aaila, this feels like, 'they are forgetting some of our traditions'. This series of small, gradual losses, may mean that once-familiar Afghan customs may eventually give way to new interests and influences.

Today, Aaila juggles two roles. She wants to preserve her heritage. She also wants to adapt to living in a new society. This balancing act brings us to our third framework: biculturalism, an approach that seeks to navigate two cultures without abandoning either.[6] To Aaila, this would be the ideal outcome of her efforts, which is why she is constantly calibrating how to raise her daughters even as she tries to find her way in a new country. Despite her medical training in Afghanistan, she and her husband have taken on jobs far removed from their expertise while she studies for a licensing exam that would allow her to practice her profession in the United States. 'We had good jobs in Afghanistan', she says. 'Now, we start over'.

I hope this discussion of assimilation, integration and biculturalism shows just how connected these frameworks are to each other. When put in dialogue with each other, they help us understand the challenges and struggles Aaila faces. That said, these frameworks also all focus on a balancing/either/or understanding of cross-cultural experiences, an approach that limits us in thinking through what a more expansive approach might be.

Third Culture Kids (TCKs), Acculturation and Intersectionality

I want to move beyond thinking about cross-cultural identities as a balancing act and invite us to think more dynamically and expansively about identity. Let's return to Marta's declaration 'I'm three times something!' to question some of the assumptions that underlie frameworks like multiculturalism, integration and assimilation. How can we start to think about our identities as exponential rather than fractional? By looking towards frameworks that allow for more fluid understanding of identity.

There are theories that can help us get there. An Indian scholar and thinker, Homi Bhabha proposes 'third space' to describe how new identities emerge at the crossroads of cultures.[7] Postcolonial literature scholar, Edward Said similarly critiques fixed categories, reminding us that identity is always shaped by history and power dynamics.[8] There are no static identities.

These insights echo the experiences of, so-called, Third Culture Kids (TCKs) and those navigating multiple cultural worlds. Coined by sociologists Ruth Hill Useem and Richard Downie, and later expanded on by Ruth Van Reken and others, the term highlights the experiences of children who navigate multiple cultural influences and create their own sense of belonging.[9] Strictly speaking, TCKs are children who grow up in cultures different from those of their parents. This leads them to develop a blended sense of identity that is distinct from their countries of origin and the countries they call home.

When I spoke to her, Hannah, a parent, shared that her children are quintessential TCKs. As Christian, American missionaries, Hannah and her family spent years in Somalia, Djibouti and Kenya. The children internalized a mix of cultural norms informed by their experiences living in these countries and attending international schools. Hannah shares that her children's identity is now layered and complex. 'My youngest feels most connected to Djibouti', Hannah explains, 'even though he looks American'.

Borrowing from Bhabha, TCKs and other cross-cultural kids (or CCKs) live in kind of 'third space' (or what they call Third Culture), as their identities and sense of belonging are shaped by exposure to different cultures. They tend to develop unique skills as a result. They are good at bridging cultural divides. They are adaptable. They have a global perspective. They also face unique challenges. They may feel rootless and struggle with long-term relationships. They may continue to meander and seek out new cultural experiences. They may resist settling down. These ongoing negotiations have been described through acculturation and intersectionality, both more contemporary approaches to understanding complex identities.[10]

Unlike more static approaches like multiculturalism, acculturation and intersectionality focus on the continuous interplay between cultural influences. 'Being a TCK is its own intersection', Sashi reflects, acknowledging how overlapping aspects of culture, language and belonging shaped their journey. For Sashi, the intersection of their TCK background and Nepali heritage often meant existing in a space where they were both insider and outsider. Thinking intersectionally also allows Sashi to account for their queerness, which adds another layer to their identity. Growing up in environments where gender roles and cultural norms were often rigid, Sashi's understanding of their queerness evolved alongside their cultural identities. 'Each place I've lived brought its own challenges and freedoms', they noted.

Moving Forward

So where do all these stories, theories and frameworks leave us when it comes to thinking about our children's identities? To answer this question, I return again and again to my experiences as a parent. Raising Marek has taught me that I need to let go of fixed ideas about his identity and mine. Instead, I need to accept that both of our identities will continue to evolve. I continue to watch him grow and see this as an invitation to rethink my notions of identity, belonging. What does it mean to feel at home in multiple worlds? How can I help him feel comfortable navigating the spaces in-between?

Marek's sense of self shifts constantly, and I've come to see this as a strength rather than a weakness. Last summer, we spent time in the Czech Republic where he was immersed in the local culture. He ate Czech food. He watched Czech TV. He went mushrooming in the forests close to his great-grandparents' village. At the end of the summer, he declared, 'I feel Czech'. Then we returned to Los Angeles and after eating at his favorite Mexican restaurant and spending a day at the beach, he told me he feels every bit an American. Sometimes, especially when he is tired, he tells me, 'I don't know what I am'. In all these moments, I just reassure him that this is all okay. He can feel he belongs to many places. He can feel conflicted. He can be confused, and he can have clarity. This is all part of his cross-cultural journey. He will get to decide how he defines himself, knowing it may change over time.

In the meantime, I share what I learned from the parents I met in writing this book: Marek needs to learn to notice the world around him. He needs to pay attention to the way a classmate asks about his lunch when they are curious that he is eating something 'different'. He should take time to note the tone a teacher uses to compliment his bilingual skills. He should learn to watch and listen, really take it all in. And he should keep an open mind. 'What do you think they're trying to say?' I ask him when he shares something that happened to him. 'What do you think they see in you? And what might they see in themselves? How might this have played out differently in a different place, a different country?'

These aren't easy questions, especially for a 10-year-old. But Marek often surprises me with his insights. Once, while visiting family in Prague, he came home from school visibly frustrated. I asked him what was wrong, and he told me about a conversation with some classmates. 'They think everyone in America is rich', he said. 'They asked me if we have a swimming pool. When I told them no, they looked so confused'.

I asked him how he felt about their questions. 'It's annoying', he admitted, 'but I think they just don't really know what it's like'. In that moment, I saw the seeds of cross-cultural insight and curiosity taking root. He was starting to navigate not just his own identity but also the assumptions others were making about him, his family and the places he calls home.

I also continue to learn and rethink my own assumptions. Marek's experiences challenge me to reflect on my own sense of identity too. As a parent, I've realized that my job isn't to pass down a fixed blueprint of what it means to be Czech, Nepali or anything else. Instead, I aim to create a space where Marek has permission to explore. I can share the stories, traditions and languages that connect me to my roots. I also need to leave room for him to make his own choices. More than anything, I have to continue to listen. Some days, this feels like a delicate balance. I want him to know his heritage deeply, but I also want him to feel free to forge new connections and embrace new influences. He needs to find his own relationships to his cultural identities, and these will be different from my own.

Raising Marek has taught me that identity isn't about choosing between cultures. Instead, I need to accept the contradictions and find joy in the intersections. I need to recognize that feeling 'Czech' one day, 'American' the next, or even 'mixed up' is all part of the journey. And it's about encouraging him, and myself, to approach these moments with curiosity and kindness, both toward ourselves and the people we meet along the way. As parents, we often think we're the ones teaching, but Marek has shown me that identity is anything but fixed.

When I think about the stories of people like Hannah, Aaila and Sashi, I'm reminded of how different cross-cultural identities can be. Hannah has raised TCKs and has accepted their unique mix of cultures. Aaila is committed to teaching her kids both Farsi and giving them the space to adjust to life in the United States. Sashi reminds us that identities are shaped by the people and places we encounter, whether at school, at home or in the communities we build.

For those of us raising cross-cultural kids, one thing is clear: our children's identities won't stay the same. They'll shift and grow with every new experience, relationship and challenge. And so will ours. And even for someone like Aaila, whose Afghan identity feels so central to her life now, there may come a time when her sense of self shifts in response to her daughters' experiences and their growing connection to a new culture. Identity, after all, is not fixed. It grows, adapts and surprises us in ways we often don't expect.

I've learned that my identity as a parent is as dynamic as my son's is as a child. His sense of self won't look exactly like mine, even though it's shaped by some of the same cultural roots. It's a realization I've had to come to gradually, and I recognize that my mother faced the same challenge. As a Czech woman raising a child with Czech and Nepali roots, she took a long time to understand that my identity would be different from hers. Similarly, my son's Czech-Nepali-Indian-American identity is different from mine.

As parents, all we can do is try to support this process of growth, even when it feels messy or uncertain. Encourage your children to explore their heritage AND leave room for them to embrace new influences. Create a home where cultural diversity isn't just acknowledged but celebrated, where it's okay to mix languages at the dinner table or to feel connected to places you have never lived in. By taking a more fluid approach, we may help our children grow into people who carry their cultures with pride while staying open to everything the world has to offer. And maybe, in the process, we'll come to better understand and embrace our own evolving identities as well.

Notes

(1) Names of all the people I interviewed and family members they mentioned have been changed to protect their identity. When needed, I also changed where they live. Furthermore, some interview quotes have been lightly edited for readability without compromising their intent and meaning.
(2) Gutmann, 1994; Kymlicka, 2000.
(3) Barry, 2001; Kymlicka, 2009; Lenard, 2016; Reitz *et al.*, 2009.
(4) Berry, 1997.
(5) Gordon, 1964.
(6) Phinney, 1990.
(7) Bhabha, 1994.
(8) Said, 1994.
(9) Useem & Downie, 1976.
(10) Crenshaw, 1991.

Takeaways from Chapter 2

Identity grows by adding, not subtracting. When kids layer new traditions, languages and friendships onto what they already know, their sense of self becomes richer. Belonging isn't about picking one identity over another.

Living between cultures brings fresh insights. Helping children navigate two (or more) worlds teaches them to see things from different angles. It can also help them take pride in the unique vantage point that comes from standing in the middle.

Thriving across cultures takes both grit and openness. By showing flexibility when it comes to cross-cultural parenting, parents can model how to adapt without losing what matters.

Identity is a living, breathing thing. As your child meets new people and tries new experiences, who they are will evolve. Parents can encourage that flow to help them grow into their fullest selves.

Blending traditions builds meaningful bonds. Whether it's cooking a family recipe, sharing stories or inventing new rituals, weaving together your cultures creates moments where kids feel truly seen and connected.

Reflection Questions – Chapter 2

Here are five reflection questions you might consider based on the themes included in this chapter:

(1) How do you perceive your own cultural identity? In what ways does it shift when you are at home, at work, traveling, or interacting with different communities?

(2) How do you currently view your children's cultural identities? In what ways do you think their identities will change as they grow older and experience different environments such as school, travel and interactions with extended family?

(3) Why is it important to you that your children develop a strong and positive cross-cultural identity? What values and benefits do you hope they gain from this experience?

(4) How do the daily realities, media communities and spaces you engage with support or hinder the expression of your family's cross-cultural identities?

(5) As your child's identity evolves, how do you balance guiding them toward cultural traditions while allowing them to explore their own path? Have you ever changed your perspective on cultural identity because of something your child has said or done?

Activity: Mapping Our Cross-Cultural Selves

Purpose and Benefits

This activity helps parents and children explore and appreciate their multiple cross-cultural identities. By mapping out and discussing these overlapping identities, families can better understand how their unique backgrounds and experiences interact and influence each other in intercultural settings and can help them foster connection and self-awareness.

Duration: Approximately 20–25 minutes

- Introduction: 2–3 minutes.
- Drawing and mapping: 13 minutes.
- Sharing and reflection: 5–7 minutes.

What You Will Need

For an analog version of the activity:

- Large sheet of paper or poster board.
- Colored markers or crayons.
- Stickers or small decorative items (optional).
- Photos or magazine cutouts (optional).

For a digital version of the activity

- A Pinterest page, Google Sheet, Canva project or other visual platform that allows for multiple users to add, annotate and edit content.

How to Do It

(1) **Introduction (2–3 minutes):**
- Explain the purpose of the activity: to explore and understand the different parts of your cultural identities and how they overlap and interact.
- Share a brief example of your own overlapping identities to model the activity.

(2) **Drawing the Central Self (3 minutes):**
- Each participant (parent and child) draws a large circle in the center of the paper to represent themselves.
- Inside the circle, write your name and a few key words or symbols that represent your core identity.

(3) **Identifying Key Aspects of Identity (5 minutes):**
- Around the central circle, draw several overlapping circles to represent different aspects of identity, such as:
  o Cultural/ethnic background (e.g. Czech, Nepali, Indian).
  o Roles (e.g. student, sibling, friend).

o Interests/hobbies (e.g. soccer player, artist, musician).
o Values/beliefs (e.g. kindness, curiosity, perseverance).
- Use markers, crayons, stickers or photos to decorate these circles.

(4) **Exploring Overlaps (5 minutes):**
- Draw lines or overlapping areas to show how different aspects of identity interact and influence each other.
- In these overlapping areas, write notes or draw symbols to describe how these identities combine in different contexts (e.g. celebrating holidays, participating in activities, interacting with friends).

(5) **Sharing and Discussing (5 minutes):**
- Take turns sharing your identity maps with each other.
- Parents can ask questions like:
  o How do you feel when you combine these different parts of your identity?
  o In which situations do you notice your identities overlapping the most?
  o Are there any new aspects of your identity you are discovering?

(6) **Reflection (2–3 minutes):**
- What did you learn about each other's identities?
- Discuss how understanding these overlapping identities can strengthen your family's connection and appreciation for each other's unique experiences.

Reflection or Follow-Up (Optional)

- How does recognizing overlapping identities change your understanding of yourself and your family?
- Are there other aspects of your identity you'd like to explore further?

3 Get on the Same Page

Figure 3.1 'It takes a village' and cross-cultural parents should talk. (credit A. Desai)

Pavel and Evelyn debate the same issue every December. When will they put up their Christmas tree in their Czech-Chinese (specifically Hong-Kong) family? For Pavel, who grew up in a small Czech village, the Christmas tree is a symbol of the season's magic. In his family, that magic didn't arrive until Christmas Eve. 'When I was a child', he reminisced when I interviewed him, 'We would go out on Christmas Eve, just before dark, to cut down the tree ourselves. It was a ritual, something we always did. The tree didn't just appear; it was brought in at the last moment. It was the grand finale after a year of waiting'.

Having grown up in Hong Kong, his wife had a different vision and timeline. For her, the Christmas tree is something that should be enjoyed throughout the entire Christmas season. The tree is not about a moment. It is a centerpiece of the warmth and festivity that defines the season, which is why it should be erected and decorated well ahead of Christmas Eve. 'Why would we wait until the last minute?' she asked, half-amused, half-bewildered, when I talked to her. 'We buy such a beautiful tree, spend hours decorating it with the children, and then we only get to enjoy it for a few days? It seems like a waste. I'd rather have it up in early December'.

The first year they were together, Pavel insisted on sticking to his tradition. The tree went up on Christmas Eve, just as it had always been done in his family. But as time went by things started to shift. The biggest shift came after their children were born and Christmas became even more important. Though they were excited about the holiday, Evelyn and Pavel's daughters didn't understand why they had to wait until the last possible moment to put up their Christmas tree. Likely encouraged by their mother (Pavel's laughing suspicion), they started to push for the tree to go up earlier each year. 'Please, Dad', they'd plead, 'can we put up the tree now? All our friends already have theirs up!'

Evelyn and Pavel's love story began far from their respective homelands. They met as students studying in Europe. Evelyn wanted to pursue a career in academia. Pavel, a Czech, wanted to experience a new approach to learning. Their relationship was defined and shaped through several relocations which they both saw as something that strengthened their bond. In fact, the challenges they faced made them more aware of the cultural expectations they each brought to the table.

And so it happened that the debates around the tree became a microcosm of their marriage, where Czech and Hong Kong cultures met, sometimes clashed and were always ultimately negotiated. 'It's our Christmas now', Pavel noted when I spoke with him. The tree may appear at a different time each year, but that is what makes it uniquely theirs. Eventually, the Christmas tree became more than a holiday ornament; it became a symbol of Pavel and Evelyn's cross-cultural family. Each year, the tree reminds them that in their home rituals reflect who they are as a family.

Pavel and Evelyn's story reflects the realities that many cross-cultural families, including mine, come to understand: parenting across cultures is not a one-time negotiation but an ongoing dialogue. Traditions, practices and even values evolve as children grow, parents change and life circumstances shift. What worked in one phase of life may no longer resonate later, just as parents' own relationships with their cultural identities can deepen, fade or transform over time. Moving to new places brings new expectations and challenges, prompting couples to reexamine their choices. They may find that a heritage language that once connected them might feel isolating in another context. They will need to respond to both internal shifts (within themselves and their family) and external ones that they cannot necessarily control.

As they navigate these uncertainties, the parents I spoke with overwhelmingly prioritize 'getting on the same page' with each other and maintaining open communication. If they decide that raising their kids with a cross-cultural outlook is important to them, they also realize that it's not just about what they do to support them. They also have to ensure that everyone involved in their children's lives understands what it means to raise a cross-cultural child. They have to be ready to defend their decision and be patient when explaining it to others.

When I decided to raise my son, Marek, multilingually, I committed to only speaking Czech to him, even if we found ourselves in an English or other language environment. I soon encountered pushback from my Indian in-laws, who felt uncomfortable (and perhaps even embarrassed) that I insisted on speaking to my son in a language that they and their family friends didn't understand. Luckily, my husband was on board with our approach and even committed to learning some Czech to make it easier for our family to communicate with each other. We both had to explain our reasoning to my in-laws multiple times. We also had to make clear that our stance was non-negotiable and that we were both committed to it. Eventually, they grasped that this was not about excluding or insulting them. We just had to stick to speaking Czech to Marek to ensure that he learned it early on. Over time, they actually even embraced the situation, and shared insights about Marek's multilingualism with the same friends, who had once been offended by our approach.

From Christmas trees to linguistic decisions, this chapter is about the decisions that parents and caregivers have to make and about the conversations they need to have as well. Of course, I can't cover all the ins and outs of cross-cultural relationships. That would be an impossible task given their complexity and uniqueness (though I hope someone will write that book too). Instead, I focus on sharing the experiences and insights shared by the parents I spoke with, along with my own reflections, to invite you to think about what you and your partner will prioritize in your own cross-cultural parenting journey.

The approach you will take in your cross-cultural parenting is deeply personal and dynamic. It will also evolve and respond to shifting realities. I hope the stories and reflections I share here lead to conversations, inspire ideas and provide reassurance that while challenges are inevitable, they are also opportunities for growth and connection.

Cultural Differences in Parenting

Cultural norms influence the way parents raise their children. In some places, parents take a more authoritative approach and emphasize structure and discipline. Others lean towards more permissive approaches that focus on emotional well-being and autonomy. An ever-growing number of books and studies now explore the many different parenting styles across the globe.

In her book *Bringing Up Bébé*, Pamela Druckerman explores the French approach to parenting. She notes that the French parents tend to emphasize independence and self-discipline. They set clear boundaries with a certain degree of freedom. They encourage children to develop self-control and patience. At the same time, they make sure that children understand the importance of rules and structure even as they are relatively free to explore their environment.[1]

Taking a similar approach, *The Danish Way of Parenting* by Jessica Joelle Alexander and Iben Dissing Sandahl provides insights into Danish parenting. The authors note that Danish parenting tends to be more relaxed and play-oriented. Danish parents want to foster emotional well-being and happiness among their children. Empathy and connection take precedence over discipline. This approach is rooted in the belief that children should be happy and well-adjusted.[2]

Scholarly work on parenting and cultural differences extends far beyond Europe. In *Parenting Across Cultures: Childrearing, Motherhood and Fatherhood in Non-Western Cultures*, contributors examine a range of global parenting practices and how these approaches are changing.[3] We learn that Kenyan communities prioritize extended family and community involvement. Japanese parents lean into a more structured and discipline-focused parenting style. Singaporean parents grapple with stress as they balance pressures of academic success with the emotional well-being of their children.

Unsurprisingly, cultural differences in parenting can become a source of tension within cross-cultural families.[4] Parents may struggle to reconcile their approaches to discipline, to emotional well-being and to educational priorities. Parents may disagree over how strictly to enforce bedtime routines. They may not see eye to eye when it comes to academic achievement or the tone they take with their children. Sakina, who was raised in South Korea, told me that these differences have led to discussions in her home as she and her French-Canadian husband figure out how to raise their two boys. Initially, Sakina insisted on integrating Korean language and culture into their home. She enrolled her two sons in a Korean preschool. She cooked Korean food. Then she realized that the boys were not learning about the French-Canadian roots from their father. She asked her husband to get more involved with their linguistic immersion. But, he seemed unable to do it. 'He just naturally switched to English', Sakina complained, 'so I had to put them in a French school because I thought I could manage the Korean part'. She then started to work on a plan that would allow her to move the whole family to Korea later on to fully immerse them in Korean culture. 'You find your footing every day', she noted.

To be clear, the complexities of cross-cultural parenting can put a strain on couples and families. The statistics and studies I reviewed reveal higher rates of marital discord and even divorce in cross-cultural marriages.[5] There can be communication barriers, cultural misunderstandings, and family pressures. All of these barriers can lead to conflict which becomes worse when partners cannot find common ground when it comes to parenting and raising their children. One partner may feel their cultural values are being marginalized. In other instances, parents may not agree on how to handle specific situations (i.e. how long a child can stay out with friends) leading to an inconsistent approach within a home. Without a strong, shared understanding and mutual respect for each other's cultural backgrounds, the stress of cross-cultural parenting can become overwhelming.[6] Over time, these unresolved issues can build up, eroding the foundation of the relationship.

Many of the parents I spoke with recognized these risks. They also knew they needed to constantly revisit their cultural priorities and approaches when it comes to parenting. They hoped that communicating and embracing compromise could help them build a parenting strategy that everyone could embrace. Sophia shared with me that she constantly checks in with her husband before making parenting decisions. Though she grew up in a Chinese household and wants to pass on this part of her heritage, she is now raising bicultural children with a non-Asian partner in the United States. 'I have to go more out of my way to really emphasize their Asian culture because it's not naturally all around us... My parents and my family aren't in-state, so it's not like people are stopping by, and it's just naturally there all the time', she explains.

Sophia grew up immersed in her Chinese heritage. 'We were exclusively pretty much eating Chinese food for every meal', she recalls. However, growing up in Michigan, she also felt the tension of balancing two cultural worlds: 'My parents were pretty strict... they were afraid you'd become "too Americanized". So, there was always a lot of push and pull, with me trying to be more like my friends and them trying to reel me back in'. This is why Sophia and her husband now consciously keep both their children's identities and practical realities in mind. They enrolled their children in Chinese language lessons and seek out opportunities to engage with Chinese traditions. 'For Chinese New Year, for example, we'll try to do something local, like make a craft at the library', she said. Yet, Sophia also acknowledges that these efforts require ongoing conversation: 'It's hard... you're constantly reassessing. How much do we focus on each culture? What works for the kids at their age?' Sophia's experience highlights how parenting across cultures is really about a dialogue between partners who also need to consider external factors that will inform their approach. In Sophia's case, 'speaking more than one language can be celebrated in one setting but might make the kids feel different in another'. This is why Sophia and her husband constantly revisit their approach.

Sometimes You Just Have to Laugh

Working on this project, I learned that humor can be an immensely powerful cross-cultural communication tool. Humor can serve as a bridge, connecting people by highlighting shared human experiences, even when language, customs or values otherwise create barriers. Humor can lighten the mood. In cross-cultural families, humor can become a way to diffuse tension, manage conflicts and foster intimacy. Light humor can help family members lighten the situation around inevitable cultural misunderstandings. A well-timed joke can break the ice during a heated argument or offer a moment of levity in a stressful situation. Humor can add lightness that gives family members permission to step back from their frustrations and see the situation from a less serious, more forgiving perspective. Sometimes you have to laugh, or you would cry.

Evelyn knows this balancing act all too well. After moving to a mid-sized Czech city, Evelyn reached to humor to cope with cultural differences and, in her words, survive. 'Humor is how I keep my sanity', she confided when I talked to her. 'When you're constantly juggling different cultures, it's easy to get frustrated. But if you can laugh about it, even just a little. It makes things so much easier'.

Evelyn's humor is influenced by living in multiple cultures. She knows that what is funny in one culture can be completely misunderstood in another, so she is careful about when and how she uses it. Somewhere along the way, her knack for humor and sharp wit led to her doing stand-up comedy. As a comedian, she draws on her life and the perils of cross-cultural marriage head-on. Here is one of her jokes: 'Cantonese is my mother tongue and my husband's mother tongue is Czech. We communicate in English because we don't want to learn each other's language. It takes a lot of effort. A lot of time. And no one knows how long the marriage is going to last'. She then added, 'We've been married for 10 years'.

Stand-up became Evelyn's creative outlet. On stage she can poke and laugh at the challenges of her bi-cultural life. She can also connect with audiences who relate to the complexities of navigating love and family across cultures. Her comedy, like her marriage, reflects the reality that cross-cultural life requires patience, adaptability and (above all) a good sense of humor.

Evelyn is not alone.

Consider the experience of comedian Sindhu Vee, a well-known British-Indian stand-up comedian. Vee, who has done shows at venues like the Apollo in London, frequently draws on her Indian upbringing and parenting style. She contrasts this with her Danish husband's more relaxed approach. She shares that she tends to be stricter; he is more indulgent. She shares this in one of her routines, 'My husband's entire parenting repertoire is "Darling, please be very, very, very happy. Here's some Lego". Meanwhile, I'm over here trying not to shout at them, but then I remember, in India, shouting is basically a form of love!' By turning differences into comedy, Sindhu entertains her audiences and creates a space where these cultural tensions can be acknowledged and laughed at. They can also be diffused and examined.

Humor can also help those raised between cultures. Marcelo Hernandez, a comedian with a mixed cultural background, reflects on the pressures of being raised by a mother from Cuba in one of his stand-up routines. He jokes, 'You can't have a bad day when your mom escaped communism'. Here Hernandez acknowledges the expectations placed on children in immigrant families. He also allows the audience to examine the intergenerational tensions this can cause.

That said, humor can be a double-edged sword. Jokes can be misunderstood. Humor can hurt and alienate especially when it relies on context and shared cultural understanding. What people in one cultural context find hilarious, might be inappropriate or even offensive to those coming from another place. Sarcasm and irony, for example, are staples of humor in many Western cultures, but these forms of humor can be confusing or misinterpreted in cultures where direct communication is valued.

Some of the parents I interviewed shared these experiences. Sophia still winces when she remembers how her classmates mocked the 'weird' Chinese food she brought to school, transforming food she loved into a source of ridicule. Veera, another parent and daughter of a Jewish-American mother and a South Asian Hindu father, remembers being teased about her last name and identity. The memory of these incidents still cuts deep decades later. So yes, humor can bridge divides, it can also weaponize cultural stereotypes. It can hurt and scar, particularly in cross-cultural contexts sensitive to policing who belongs and who does not.

Even so, humor can also challenge these stereotypes and enhance understanding across cultures.[7] I admit I am a huge fan of the Canadian sitcom *Kim's Convenience*. To me this show does an excellent job of critiquing cultural stereotypes. It pokes at them. It also celebrates the experiences of an immigrant Korean family living in Canada. The character of Mr Kim ('Appa') often embodies traditional values, yet his blunt honesty and humorous misunderstandings invite viewers to reflect on generational and cultural divides. In one episode, Mr Kim playfully critiques his daughter Janet's modern attitudes while struggling to navigate the evolving social norms around gender and identity. His commentary, though rooted in his cultural background, is softened by humor. Appa is proud of his Korean heritage and his comical, yet tender, attempts to connect with his Canadian-born children highlight the universality of family dynamics. The audience is invited to laugh *with* him rather than at him. *Kim's Convenience* successfully reclaims and normalizes often misunderstood cultural characteristics. Through all this, the show uses humor to engage immigrant experiences, turning what might otherwise be sources of discomfort into moments of shared connection.

To use humor effectively in cross-cultural settings, we need to find common ground. We need to come up with jokes that both partners and family members can appreciate, even if they laugh for different reasons. To Evelyn, humor is a vital tool. 'Stand-up helped me process the frustrations', she said. 'It's the little things and learning to laugh at them instead of letting them annoy you. This can make a big difference'. Humor can connect or divide, depending on how it is used. When approached with sensitivity, humor can help us navigate cross-cultural relationships. A willingness to laugh can help families not only survive but thrive as they blend traditions, values and perspectives.

Blending Traditions

Finding common ground and blending traditions in a cross-cultural relationship can be about creating a new, shared culture that reflects the unique identities of both partners. Being intentional in creating a space for these exchanges ahead of time is helpful. Hindsight can also bring clarity. Jana, a Czech woman married to an American, reflected on this with a mix of fondness and regret when I spoke to her about how she raised her now adult children. She told me she wishes she and her husband had been more deliberate about blending their cultures and considering how those traditions would show up in their home. Things turned out ok (great actually), she shared, but being more intentional would have helped her and her husband be clear on their priorities when it came to shaping their children's identities and thinking about bilingualism.

Life can get busy, and cross-cultural elements can fade if they are not prioritized. While love and good intentions can carry families far, the subtle, everyday decisions shape how children experience their identities. We have to decide whether to speak a heritage language at home, whether to celebrate cultural holidays or whether to prioritize certain traditions. For Jana, this realization came as her children grew older and began to ask questions about the parts of their Czech heritage.

I know this balancing act well. Growing up between Czech and Nepali cultures, my parents blended our holidays. In our home, Tihar, the Hindu festival of lights, connected to Christmas. On the one hand, I still remember the contrast between the two: Tihar, with its family gatherings, oil lamps and the tradition of honoring dogs, cows and crows, was a communal celebration that I shared with my extended Nepali family. Christmas was all about the cookies, the tree (which appeared on Christmas Eve at our house), the presents, Czech carols and calling my grandparents. Christmas was a private, almost sacred, space where my parents and I adhered to Czech traditions in ways that contrasted the bustle of the Tihar celebrations. On the other hand, the holidays blended in our house as the lights that define Tihar also stayed around for Christmas, as did the sense that we could be extra generous to each other. As a child, I always thought I got to experience the best of both worlds.

This experience of blending two seemingly different holidays taught me that cultural traditions don't need to compete; instead, they can build on one another, creating something unique and meaningful. For many cross-cultural families, it's also about making space for more than one culture to exist in the home. Blending traditions isn't just about preserving the past; it's also about creating something new together. We have an opportunity to weave rich cultures into our daily lives, ensuring our children feel connected through food, bedtime rituals or celebrations. We can forge routines that are unique to our families.

Have the Conversation

The success of relationships and parenting, however, doesn't rest solely on these new traditions. It is also deeply rooted in the ongoing conversations parents commit to having with each other. All the parents I spoke to agreed that cross-cultural parenting is a dynamic process, one that requires constant adaptation as children grow and circumstances change.

Catherine, an American who grew up in Nepal, and her Canadian husband, have ongoing conversations about cultural identity as they raise their children in Belize. Catherine believes in immersing their children in the local culture. She also wants them to know about their American and Canadian roots. 'We wanted them to feel at home here, in the country where they were growing up, but also aware of the cultural histories of the places they come from', she explains.

To maintain this balance, Catherine and her husband frequently revisit their parenting strategies. They want to make sure they are aligned, especially when it comes to fostering a connection to their children's diverse backgrounds. 'One reason we moved here was to give our kids an international experience', she said. 'We wanted them to have exposure to a different worldview'. But children grow and new needs arise. As her children's identities shift, Catherine and her husband continue to have the conversation. Most recently she was surprised to learn that despite having US citizenship, her daughter insisted that she does not feel American. Hearing this, Catherine and her husband realized that they needed to think more deeply about their children's ties to the United States, which was something they had always taken for granted.

Ultimately, we (as parents) must commit to having the conversation. Again. And again. It is really best if both partners engage in this dialogue. Talking can help families navigate their cultural differences. It can align their parenting strategies. Whether informed by a personal experience, a book, a movie or a stand-up comedy routine, these conversations can help foster a sense of shared purpose within the family. They can also help create a family environment that respects and integrates everyone's backgrounds.

Jana, whom I mentioned earlier, had this advice to share, 'Have that conversation with your partner and understand where they are coming from when it comes to raising mixed kids. I was just in love. So, we did not have this conversation. It worked out, but still. Have that conversation. Talk about how you want to organize things and how you are going to handle cultural differences when they come up'. As cross-cultural parents, we need to be proactive in discussing what we value and what we want out of our family life. What cultural traditions matter to us? How can we make sure we are listening to each other?

So, discuss your background and culture with your partner. Be clear about why parenting across cultures matters to you. I know they say love conquers all, but having the conversation can also help.

Notes

(1) Druckerman, 2012.
(2) Alexander & Sandahl, 2016.
(3) Selin, 2013.
(4) Craft et al., 2022.
(5) Romano, 2008.
(6) Benet-Martínez & Haritatos, 2005.
(7) Hall J., 2013.

Takeaways from Chapter 3

Creating new rituals strengthens your bond. When you blend traditions and invent ceremonies, you're not just celebrating culture. You are building memories that belong uniquely to your family.

Honest conversations keep you in sync. Talking through your values and expectations helps you navigate differences, so you stay united as your children grow and change.

A little laughter goes a long way. Finding the humor in cultural mix-ups and family quirks turns tension into connection and makes everyday moments more joyful.

Mixing parenting styles brings harmony. Adapting rules, routines and learning approaches to honor each heritage lets you craft a home life that meets your kids' needs while respecting both worlds.

Embracing the messiness deepens closeness. Accepting that cross-cultural parenting is a work in progress means using each challenge as a chance to learn, grow and draw your family even tighter together.

Reflection Questions – Chapter 3

Here are five reflection questions you might consider based on the themes included in this chapter:

(1) How do you feel about your cultural background? What traditions do you want to pass on to your children?

(2) How do you and your partner decide which traditions you will prioritize in your home? How have you and your partner adapted or blended your cultural traditions? Are there any new family traditions that have emerged as a result?

(3) Humor can help families engage their cultural differences. Can you think of a time when humor helped you handle a cultural misunderstanding or eased tension in your family? Have you come across a comedian, TV series or meme that humorously captures the challenges of crossing cultures?

(4) How do your cultural backgrounds influence your parenting styles? Are there specific areas (i.e. discipline, education or emotional expression) where you and your partner's approaches differ? How have you worked through these differences?

(5) How often do you and your partner discuss cultural values and parenting strategies? Have you ever used media (think documentaries, news articles, YouTube videos) to start discussions about cultural identity or family values?

Activity: Family Culture Conversations

Purpose and Benefits

This activity invites parents to reflect on the cultural values and traditions they wish to pass on to children. It promotes open communication, encourages collaboration in blending cultural practices and uses humor to create a relaxed environment for discussing important, and sometimes sensitive, topics.

Duration: Approximately 30–45 minutes

- Reflection: 5–10 minutes.
- Comedy clip: 5–10 minutes.
- Group discussion: 15–20 minutes.

What You Will Need

- Pen and paper (or a digital note-taking tool) for listing traditions or values.
- Access to a short clip about cross-cultural experiences (e.g. Sindhu Vee, Marcelo Hernandez).
- A comfortable space for group discussion.

How to Do It

(1) **Start with Reflection:**
Take a few moments to list 1–2 cultural traditions or values you and your family members consider most important for the children to experience. These could include holiday traditions, family rituals, food customs or values like respect or education.

(2) **Watch and Laugh:**
Watch a short comedy clip together, focusing on cross-cultural experiences. Note how humor might help you and your family explore how cultural differences shape everyday life, parenting styles or family dynamics.

(3) **Discuss Together:**
- Reflect on the clip and discuss how humor helps navigate cultural differences.
- Transition to a broader conversation about the values and traditions you each listed, highlighting overlaps and differences.

(4) **Set a Goal:**
Work together to choose one cultural practice or tradition to reinforce in your family. Examples include a special meal, a holiday tradition or a weekly storytelling session.

Reflection or Follow-Up (Optional)

- What did you learn about each other's cultural priorities?
- Did humor help facilitate the conversation?
- What steps can you take to ensure the chosen tradition becomes a regular part of your family life?

Part 2
Bridge with Media and Popular Culture

4 By Any Media

Figure 4.1 Think about both old and new media as tools that can help. (credit A. Desai)

In 2015, we introduced baby Marek to his great-grandmother, 'Amma', in Baroda, India. She was too old to travel to us, and we were unable to visit India so soon after his birth. We also knew that she was frail and weren't sure how long she would still be with us. So, we coordinated with one of Amma's local relatives to set up a video call. This way she would be able to see Marek, which was something we couldn't do during our regular phone calls with her.

I still tear up when I remember the moment when we held Marek up to the screen so Amma could see him more closely. Her eyes lit up. She smiled and got emotional. She whispered blessings to him in Gujarati, her tone filled with love and pride. She told him he would grow up strong and be happy. She cried a little and so did we. Though separated by continents, we were connected. It almost felt like she was able to reach out across the miles to touch his tiny hand.

To help Amma connect with Marek, we also printed out photos of him and created photo albums that we sent to her through another relative. We later learned that Amma cherished these photos. She held them. She ran her fingers over them. She showed them all to her visitors and introduced Marek to many people he has yet to meet. Sadly, Amma passed away within a year of Marek's birth. They were never able to meet in person. And though connecting over FaceTime and via photographs could never replace her holding him, I remain grateful for these moments of connection.

Old and new media are incredibly important when it comes to building and maintaining cultural connections. As a cross-cultural parent, I constantly reach for digital media. I read blog posts. I scroll through social media. I use FaceTime to connect with family. The parents I met through this book do the same. They listen to podcasts. They create digital photo albums. They stream video. Yet, these same parents also value more traditional forms of media like books, letters and photographs. If digital media provide convenience and immediacy, more traditional media tends to endure. It can be held and treasured. It may be best if we think about media as a toolkit, which enables us to create and consume content even as we connect across a distance.

In this chapter I focus on media. I explore how it has evolved. I touch on how it continues to transform and how the parents I met use it to support their parenting. Drawing on my own experiences, I share how taking a by any media approach can help us navigate a fast-changing media landscape to support rich, cross-cultural experiences for our children.[1]

Media is Always in Transition

Media is, and has long been, in transition. Media scholar Henry Jenkins places these changes on a timeline that focuses on what content is shared and how it is received. Old media may fade into oblivion. It may also resurface and find new life in new media contexts. The case of the record player and boom box are a case in point. They are older media that are still around today. We no longer use them in the same ways, but we may have found new applications for them. Building on this observation, Jenkins also invites us to think about how old and new media intersect with each other and transform.[2] Dance was once limited to live performance venues. Now, it dominates social media platforms like TikTok allowing dancers to reach audiences they would have not even dreamed about a few decades ago.

Social movement scholar Jennifer Earl also helps us make sense of media change. Earl distinguishes between 'scale' change and 'model' changes in media. She compares 'scale change' in media getting a car with a bigger and stronger engine.[3] The improved engine allows you to travel further and faster without fundamentally altering how it works. Model change would be going from a car fueled by gas to a high-speed train, bus or even bicycle, signaling that a fundamental change has taken place.

Thinking about the last century of media, the fax machine could be seen as a scale change moment in our ability to transmit documents. The untethering of communication ushered in via the mobile phone would be a moment of model change, ending the era of the corded phone.

Understanding media as always in transition helps us recognize that while the media tools we use may change, our approach to how we think about them can remain constant.[4]

Media is Here to Stay

Even a cursory look at the parenting shelf of any bookstore quickly confirms that media, especially social media, is top of mind for parents today. I tried, but ultimately failed, to keep track of the many books that address the impact of media on children's development. Some of these books highlight the need for balanced screen time. Others hone in on the importance of age-appropriate content. Still others warn us about the mental health implications of excessive social media use for tweens and teens. And yes, of course, there are real and legitimate reasons to be concerned about the role of media in our daily lives. We should be worried about online privacy. We should, as sociologist Jonathan Haidt argues, take the psychological impact of constantly comparing oneself to others on some social media platforms seriously.[5] We should be worried about disinformation and pornography. Many parents, including me, do worry about navigating 'screen time' management, online safety and cyberbullying.

At the same time, I believe that monitoring screen time is an incredibly blunt and largely ineffective tool for navigating children's engagement with media. As anthropologist Susan Kresnicka pointed out in a blog conversation I had with her in 2020, 'screens' are just a piece of hardware. I would add that 'time' measures duration and tells us nothing about what is actually taking place. Clearly, we need more nuanced approaches to understanding media. And we need them now more than ever as media shows up in almost every facet of our children's lives.

In the COVID-19 summer of 2020, I got quite excited about the possibilities of online interest-based learning for young children when my then five-year-old son took classes through Outschool, a company offering class-like experiences online (outschool.com). The classes (taught over Zoom) were generally small (ranging from 4–6 kids) and short (15–30 minutes over several days or weeks). The offerings were staggeringly diverse, with classes on almost any topic imaginable (from butterflies to photography, from drawing superheroes to learning French). While somewhat uneven because some instructors were more experienced than others, the classes all helped my son connect learning to a subject area that interested him. He learned a lot and enjoyed it.

Perhaps it was this positive experience that made the first days of distance-learning kindergarten such a shock in Fall 2020. Responding to critiques of how distance learning happened in public schools that spring, California passed legislation mandating the duration of instruction for every grade level. For kindergarten, it was 180 minutes. To meet this mandate, my son's school leaned into 'screentime' and implemented a three-hour Zoom call which the teacher had to fill with programming. Seeing my son stare vacantly at the screen as his one teacher attempted and (understandably) failed to engage her 24 students, I couldn't help but think that there must be better ways to do this.

This experience inspired me to reimagine how technology could support learning and led me to search for alternative online learning experiences for Marek. I discovered that one-on-one online language classes work extremely well for him, offering an interactive and personalized approach that captures his attention and allows him to thrive. Today, he continues to learn Czech, Spanish and French this way. He is developing his skills through personalized one-on-one learning instruction. More recently, he has also been experimenting with using AI as a language tutor by asking it to generate and test him on vocabulary. Both of these experiences have reinforced for me that media, like online learning, is just a tool. We have to choose how to use it. When used thoughtfully, it can help students learn and connect, but without care, it can disconnect more than it connects.

Still, many parenting and media books still deploy a rather narrow definition of media, often reducing it to concepts like 'screentime'. They also tend to focus on the child as the user of media and not the parent–child relationship as central to any sustainable approach to media and parenting. Here are a few books in this space that illustrate this point. Lisa Guernsey takes a deep dive into early childhood and television viewing in her book *Screen Time*.[6] While more nuanced, Anya Kamenetz's *The Art of Screen Time* still concludes that kids should 'Enjoy Screens. Not too much. Mostly with others'.[7] While helpful in some ways, these books fall short when it comes to providing parents with a longer-term approach to parenting with media even as the media environments around us continue to change.

To be clear, there are scholars and practitioners engaging with this question in thoughtful and helpful ways. In a refreshing take, Katie Davis draws on her experiences as a parent and media scholar to provide a more constructive helpful approach to media/screen time in her book *Technology's Child*. Pushing past 'time', she urges parents to ask two key questions:

(1) Is your child's media experience self-directed? Are they in the 'driver's seat' and 'calling the shots'? In other words, ask yourself whether your children have a sense of agency when it comes to the media they are using.

(2) And, is this experience community-supported? Here Davis urges us to think about whether they are connecting with others in healthy and supportive ways when they engage with media.[8]

To me, Davis addresses questions surrounding digital media head-on – pushing us to ask about the context and connections that surround children's engagement with it. And with the advent of artificial intelligence, the need to address questions around moments of media in transition become ever more urgent.

Still, for better or worse, media is here to stay. A media-free world is nearly impossible to imagine, making fear-mongering and guilting around media unhelpful approaches for parents. As the LA Times article 'Parents are ditching screen time limits for kids against expert advice' points out, most families were not adhering to screen time recommendations even before the COVID-19 pandemic.[9] The 2020 Common Sense Media Census found that children were watching significant amounts of digital media daily, with little concern from parents about potential negative effects.[10] In fact, many parents believe that screen time offers benefits such as helping their children learn to read, boosting creativity and improving social skills. This is why it is essential to recognize that media, in its various forms, is integrated into our lives. Our focus should be on managing it wisely and recognizing where it can really help us rather than engaging in a futile exercise of eliminating it altogether.

Introducing By Any Media

For many of the parents I met, media is a powerful tool, which helps them bridge distances and maintain connections. Daria, an Iranian-American I spoke with, noted that digital tools like Google Translate allowed her to reconnect with her grandmother in Iran after years of limited communication. 'When I got pregnant, I started writing letters to my grandmother using Google Translate. She loved them, and though she couldn't write back, she'd reference what I wrote when we talked. It felt transformative for both of us'. Other parents pointed to the enduring value of more traditional and face-to-face media. As one anonymous survey respondent shared, 'In-person cultural information access is paramount and is much more focused on cultural events, books, representative toys, and creating welcoming space in our children's schools. We do not know any other multicultural families in our community, and a lot of the work we have to do is trying to make our children's school more inclusive. We are very much the sole walking ambassadors of multiculturalism in our community, as I assume most very multiracial, multicultural families are, and the in-person elements are vastly greater and more challenging'.

As a media scholar, I think about media both broadly and specifically. To do this, my colleagues and I developed an approach through our work with youth, which provides a practical framework for cross-cultural families.[11] I use *by any media* to refer to a wide range of choices and actions that tap the affordances of various media formats. I also think about media content and the meaningful relationships we share with each other around that content in our everyday lives. *By any media* encourages parents to assess their context and use all available digital, traditional and creative media resources to share cultural narratives and maintain connections. Focusing on our agency (what we can do) in navigating the media around us enables us to make choices based on our realities, possibilities and priorities. Media is not simply something we passively consume; it is also something we actively *create* and *do*.

Meet Layla

Take the case of Layla. Originally from Egypt, Layla and her husband moved to the United States 14 years ago. They are raising their three school-aged children (aged 13, 10 and 4). During the week, the older children attend a local public school and are immersed in American culture, which is why Layla makes it a priority to connect all her children to Egyptian culture.

Layla uses various media to support her children's cross-cultural upbringing. For instance, the family watches Egyptian TV shows, which offer Layla an opportunity to introduce cultural nuances into the conversation. 'Through trial and error, I discovered that funny shows are particularly effective in getting my boys' attention', Layla shares. Watching TV together has become a family activity, even as the boys struggle to understand the language given the differences between Egyptian dialect and standard Arabic. Nevertheless, Layla feels the boys catch something, and she and her husband fill in the cultural nuances, allowing this shared family time to become a bit of an 'educational experience' that connects them to their Egyptian heritage.

Layla has also tried to introduce her children to the media she grew up with, but the poor quality of older videos led her to rely on newer content which she finds less appealing but necessary. For example, she uses Shahid, an Arabic streaming service similar to Netflix, which features Arabic TV series. While these shows are different from those she watched growing up, they provide family-oriented content that Layla uses to teach her children about cultural norms and behaviors such as showing respect to elders. 'We focus on the family-oriented ones. If they see, for example, a son interacting with his father or mother or grandparents, they learn how to say hello properly and show respect'.

Weekly interactions with the Egyptian community, such as potlucks or inviting people over, provide opportunities for the children to play with other Egyptian-origin kids. 'These gatherings often feature Egyptian foods, which I see as a great connection to the culture', Layla explains. She also tries to immerse them in cultural activities related to Ramadan or Eid by bringing traditions and cooking specific foods.

To further their linguistic and cultural education, Layla has enrolled her children in Arabic classes taught from Egypt, which are more affordable and online, a trend that has boomed with COVID-19. Additionally, Layla is experimenting with Sunday schools for Islamic and Arabic studies, which can be associated with the mosque or independent organizations. Her son, preferring in-person learning over online classes, traded a one-hour Arabic class for four hours of Sunday school. 'He rebelled against online Arabic learning because it's already hard for him and he hates Zoom', she laughed.

Communication with their grandparents in Egypt is another crucial aspect of their upbringing. The children have regular video and voice calls with their grandparents via Facebook Messenger, allowing them to share their thoughts freely. These weekly calls typically last around 10 minutes and provide a valuable connection to their heritage. 'They get to talk about things they might not share with us. Their grandparents are willing listeners', Layla notes.

Layla tries to visit Egypt every year, staying with the grandparents. This living arrangement helps the children feel at home. 'In the first week, they're fine. Then they start to misbehave, which shows they feel at home', she chuckles. Despite not living in Egypt, the children have developed an affinity for Egyptian soccer player Mohamed Salah, feeling a connection to him and caring about his performance. Layla supports her children's cross-cultural upbringing, blending old and new media to create a rich, multifaceted connection to their Egyptian heritage while they grow up in the United States.

By Any Media

Layla and other cross-cultural parents I met are parenting *by any media*. That is, they use the media they have available to accomplish their cross-cultural parenting goals. They join groups on social media to get their hands on hard-to-find foreign language children's books. They organize music nights in their homes to perform live renditions of the songs on their Spotify lists for their family and friends. They enroll their kids in online language courses and download international educational apps. From streaming documentaries to mailing books across countries, from online cooking tutorials to shopping at the neighborhood international foods shop, these parents are finding creative approaches to making a cross-cultural upbringing meaningful, engaging and connected. The survey I fielded[12] confirms that parents move between in-person and online media to support cross-cultural parenting.

On the one hand, parents highly value in-person activities for helping their children connect with multiple cultures. A striking 74% of parents say these activities are 'very important' (40%) or 'extremely important' (34%). This shows that parents really believe in the power of direct, hands-on experiences to immerse their kids in different cultures. Popular activities include eating and cooking diverse foods, reading books from other cultures, traveling, attending multicultural events, participating in cultural festivals and joining community programs that celebrate various cultures.

That said, digital media is also a key tool for these parents, and 49% of parents rate associated activities as 'very important' (37%) or 'extremely important' (12%). Watching online videos (87%), accessing films from different cultures online (78%) and using social media to learn about cultural diversity are all popular activities and support virtual cross-cultural experiences. Additionally, online language classes and educational websites offering cultural content are also frequently used. These digital tools are flexible and offer a wide range of content, making them very useful in today's mediated world, as parents often combine both in-person and digital methods to enhance their children's cultural experiences. Many encourage their kids to attend after-school language classes (62%) and be part of culturally diverse school environments (45%) while also using digital resources like online games and ebooks from various cultures.

I categorized the media activities the parents engaged in into four quadrants based on prevalence (high or low) and engagement (high or low). I determined prevalence by looking at the percentage of respondents who indicated that they do this activity regularly. I defined engagement qualitatively based on the time and effort typically required for each activity. I also reclassified the activities to ensure balanced distribution across all quadrants (see Figure 4.2).

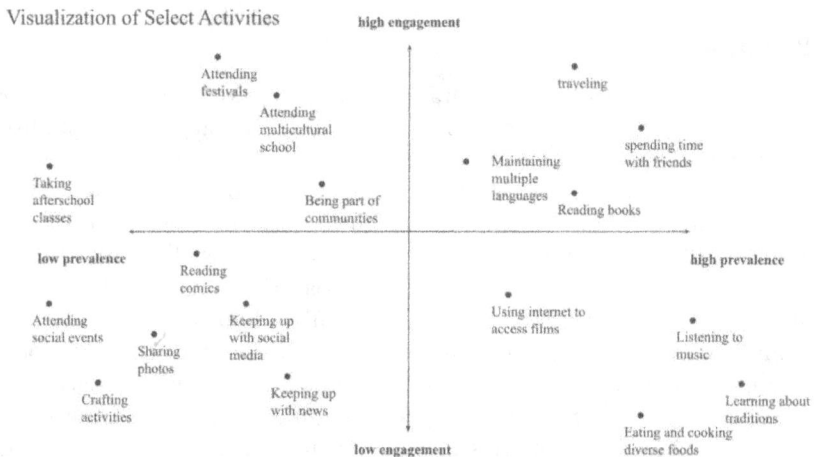

Visualization of Select Activities

Figure 4.2 This chart illustrates how surveyed cross-cultural parents use media

So, what did I notice?

- **High Prevalence/High Engagement**: Activities like 'Spending time with culturally diverse friends' and 'Traveling' fall into this quadrant. These activities are both popular and require significant time, effort and sometimes money. They involve active participation and meaningful interaction.
- **High Prevalence/Low Engagement**: These are commonly practiced activities that require relatively less effort. They include 'Eating and cooking diverse foods' and 'Using the internet to access films'. 'Listening to music' and 'Learning about traditions'.
- **Low Prevalence/High Engagement**: Activities such as 'Taking after-school classes', 'Crafting Activities' and 'Attending a multicultural school' fall into this quadrant. These activities, while less common, require significant time and effort, offering in-depth engagement with different cultures.
- **Low Prevalence/Low Engagement**: These are activities that are neither commonly practiced nor highly engaging. They include 'Sharing photos', 'Keeping up with news' and 'Reading comics'. These activities might be niche or less integrated into participants' regular routines.

What I also noticed immediately was the mix of media that parents use, confirming the *by any media* approach that parents like Layla are taking. The cross-cultural parents I surveyed value direct, hands-on experiences, cooking diverse foods, traveling and attending cultural festivals. They recognize that such activities are important when it comes to fostering cultural immersion. At the same time, they use digital tools to provide flexible, wide-ranging cultural content, from streaming documentaries to using online language classes and educational websites.

Challenges and Coping Strategies

So far, I have focused on how media can help parents who parent across media. But, I would be remiss if I didn't mention the challenges that some parents faced in navigating media with their children. I also want to share their coping strategies.

Representation: Filling in the gaps

Some parents I interviewed mentioned that finding media that reflects cross-cultural experiences can be difficult as mainstream media content rarely captures the nuanced realities of multicultural families. This leaves parents scrambling and children without role models who truly reflect their lived experiences. Layla mentioned this when I spoke with her: 'It's hard to find shows or books that reflect both Egyptian and American cultures.' Most of the time, the content is very one-dimensional and doesn't really resonate with our family's experiences. To try to make up for this, Layla seeks out Egyptian shows (from Egypt) that she can stream for her children. Although these shows don't always align with her own childhood media experiences, she uses them as starting points for discussion. She provides her children with cultural context as they watch.

Access: Barriers and resources

Some parents had a hard time accessing culturally relevant media because of geographic restrictions, paywalls or other availability. While annoying, these barriers also inspired other parents to find innovative solutions. This was the case for Benjamin, who is raising his Austrian-Nepali children in Austria and whose family has an interest in Japanese culture. He has trouble finding high-quality Nepali and Japanese content: 'Many resources are behind paywalls or not available in our region, which makes it challenging to teach our kids about their heritage'. Despite these hurdles, Benjamin and his wife find ways to connect their children to their cultural backgrounds. They make it a point to attend local community events, including Nepali film screenings. They also tap their extended networks to access content and share materials they have with other families.

Time: Constraints and juggles

Amit's family is trilingual and keeping up with everything can be a challenge. Juggling cross-cultural and linguistic priorities can feel almost impossible given his children's busy schedules. 'With school, homework and extracurriculars, it's tough to find time for additional cultural lessons. We try to fit in language practice and cultural activities, but it's a constant juggling act', he explains. Still, Amit and his wife try to work at least some elements into their daily lives. At home, they intentionally code-switch and alternate between English, Marathi and Bengali. They also use family meals to share stories about their culture and encourage their children to practice their languages in small, dare I say 'bite-sized' ways.

Cost: Stretch and contract

Immersion in cultural activities often costs money. Online classes may be behind paywalls. Books need to be ordered. Streaming services can be subscription-based. When I spoke with her, Seema described the balancing act she faces: 'We want to give our children access to their heritage, but activities like language classes, cultural events, and travel can add up quickly'. That said, some parents also branch out and find creative solutions. Seema has found ways to make cultural activities more affordable. She seeks out community events and resources, which are often free. This includes a potluck organized by a local cultural association. By combining these lower-cost options with occasional larger investments in cross-cultural experiences, Seema ensures her children can engage deeply with their heritage without overextending the family budget.

Prejudice: Barriers and resilience

Some of the parents I spoke with shared painful moments when they experienced cultural prejudice and discrimination. Sujata told me about the criticism she faced when she committed to teaching her child Tamil. She was even told that focusing on English would serve her child better. Another parent shared that their children were singled out for being different. Yet, these moments of bias also strengthened these parents' resolve to persist. 'It's a lot of work', Sujata explained, 'but I've built a parallel school at home using books, songs and DVDs to teach my son about our traditions'. She remains committed to her child's bilingual and bicultural journey and refuses to give in to the challenges she faces.

Leveraging Media for Connection

The parents I met are aware of the challenges they face. They are also aware of the opportunities. Libraries, online forums and free resources can help them overcome access barriers. Integrating cultural activities into daily routines helps parents mitigate time pressures. All in all, the experiences parents shared with me reflect a larger truth: the challenges cross-cultural parents face are inseparable from the rewards.

Taking a *by any media* approach to curating their media experience helps parents find a flexible approach that works for them and their families. They can take inventory of all the media resources available to them. They may be digital, traditional or creative. Their local libraries may offer free classes or materials. They can also join online forums where parents share cultural content. They may also look into ways to integrate short 'cultural moment' sessions into their daily routines. They may also seek supportive in-person and online communities. More on all this later.

Last summer, I watched my son read a letter I had written to my grandparents when I was his age. As he giggled at my handwriting, I was struck by the enduring power of a handwritten letter. I noticed that the younger version of myself had struggled to write in Czech. My letter was littered with small grammatical mistakes and 'Czechlish' word choices.

Still, I was able to share my life with my grandmother. I had written that my dog had died and that I had attended a cousin's wedding. My everyday life and poignant events were preserved on those pages.

Later that day we took a walk, and Marek borrowed my phone. He proceeded to take photos of everything we saw (the trees, the flowers), and created an almost minute-by-minute virtual memory of our shared moment. And yet, the letter we had read together earlier that day did something that digital media didn't. It was a material memory, one that transported my son and me to the moment when I wrote it years ago. Both formats have their place in our cross-cultural journey. Ultimately, it's not about choosing one medium over another but recognizing that each brings its own advantages. Together, they offer rich opportunities to build bridges across generations, geographies and cultures.

Notes

(1) Jenkins *et al.*, 2016.
(2) Jenkins, 2006.
(3) Earl, 2018.
(4) Jenkins, 2006.
(5) Haidt, 2024.
(6) Guernsey, 2012.
(7) Kamenetz, 2018.
(8) Davis, 2023.
(9) Gold, 2024.
(10) Rideout & Robb, 2020.
(11) Jenkins *et al.*, 2016.
(12) The survey was fielded via a number of channels from April 2023–July 2023 with a total number of 94 respondents.

Takeaways for Chapter 4

Media bridges distance and time. Whether it's a tattered postcard or a late-night video chat, parents turn to all kinds of media to help kids stay close to family and heritage, even when loved ones are oceans away.

Connection guides how we use screens. Yes, worries about screen time, privacy and misinformation are real. But, parents can also lean into what media can do to create shared moments that deepen understanding and belonging.

Old and new tools both matter. From the tactile joy of handwritten letters to the instant thrill of a FaceTime call, combining traditions with digital tools gives kids a richer taste of their roots.

Doing media side by side strengthens bonds. Streaming a favorite cultural film together, following a family recipe step-by-step in a cooking video or tackling an online language class as a team turns learning into lasting memories.

Media is here for the long haul. Rather than fight its presence, parents can integrate media thoughtfully into their daily lives. They can do this by focusing on how media can expand cultural connections instead of simply trying to limit 'screen time'.

Reflection Questions – Chapter 4

Here are five reflection questions you might consider based on the themes included in this chapter:

(1) What forms of media (books, movies, TV shows, social media, messaging apps, etc.) do you currently use with your children?

(2) Think about the types of media you rely on today. Do they mostly come from your own background, or are they a mix of influences? How do these choices shape your children's understanding of culture?

(3) Using the engagement/prevalence framework from this chapter, where do your current media practices fall? How do your experiences align with or differ from what other cross-cultural parents have reported?

(4) What challenges do you currently face in using media to support your child's cultural identity? Are there gaps in representation, accessibility or content that you notice?

(5) How has media either reinforced or helped you navigate biases and stereotypes in your child's cultural learning?

Activity: Mapping our Media Selves

Purpose and Benefits:

This activity helps families reflect on their media habits, identify shared and individual practices, and explore how media can foster joy, connection and cultural understanding. By creating visual media maps, family members can better understand the role media plays in their lives and find ways to balance individual and shared experiences.

Duration: 15–30 minutes

- Mapping: 10–15 minutes.
- Discussion and reflection: 10–15 minutes.

What You Will Need

- A piece of paper for each family member.
- Colored markers or crayons.

How to Do It

(1) Set the Time Frame:
- Decide on a time frame for mapping media habits. This could be a single day, a few days or up to a week. The goal is to capture a typical range of media usage.

(2) Draw Your Media Map:
- You each get a piece of paper and markers.
- Draw a large circle in the center of the paper and write your name inside it.
- Around the central circle, draw smaller circles to represent different types of media you use. Use different colors to differentiate between:
  - o Old media (e.g. books, letters, newspapers).
  - o New media (e.g. social media, streaming services, video calls).
- Inside each smaller circle, write the specific media tools or platforms you use (e.g. WhatsApp, Netflix, family photo albums).

(3) Visualize Your Media Habits:
- Use symbols or color codes to represent:
  - o Media that gives you joy (e.g. a smiley face or heart).
  - o Media that connects you to others (e.g. a handshake or double line connecting circles).
  - o Media that connects you to other cultures (e.g. a globe or flag).

(4) Compare Your Maps:
- Lay out all the maps together and discuss similarities and differences.

- Talk about the media practices you share and engage in as a family.
- Identify media activities unique to each person and what they gain from them.

(5) Reflect on Your Findings:

- Discuss how shared media practices strengthen your family connections.
- Talk about individual media habits and how they contribute to joy and cultural connection.
- Consider ways to include more shared media experiences that bring joy and deepen cultural understanding.

(6) Wrap Up:

- Take a photo of your media maps as a reminder of your family's habits and connections.
- Use this activity to think about how to balance individual and shared media experiences to enhance cross-cultural connections.

Reflection or Follow-Up (Optional)

- What media activities bring the most joy and connection to your family?
- How can you incorporate more shared media experiences into your routine?

5 Connect Through Popular Culture

Figure 5.1 Parents use popular culture to support their cross-cultural children. (credit A. Desai)

When his Indian-American kids were small, Amit made it a point to cue up Tamil and Hindi songs when they were in the car. He kept at it until listening to South Asian music became synonymous with commuting. Eventually his kids took over and used the time to discover Bollywood and other Indian songs through YouTube's autoplay feature. This curiosity led them to other formats. 'At some point, they went on a Shah Rukh Khan binge and then got hooked on shows like *Ms. Marvel* on Disney+', Amit shared when I talked to him. For Amit and his family exploring playlists and diving into films and TV series are moments that help them connect with each other and their cultural backgrounds.

When Amit shared these experiences with me, I felt like he had taken a page out of my playbook, as curating car-ride playlists is also something I do to introduce my son to music from other cultures. I will play a Nepali song, followed by a Czech hit or a Spanish song and confuse the YouTube algorithm in the process. Over time, these songs connect us and open up conversations about music genres and cultural context.

In much the same way, Ms. Marvel, helped Amit's children explore their Indian-American identity. The show follows Kamala Khan, a Pakistani-American teenager, who lives in suburban America as she discovers her superpowers. Kamala lives in a cross-cultural home with South Asian food, festivals and even some Bollywood stars. She crosses languages, religions and cultures, making her experience very relatable to Amit's children.

Like Amit, many of the parents I met use films, music and other popular media to introduce their children to other cultures that may or may not be familiar to them. From catchy dance moves to laughing at comedy, popular culture becomes a tool for them as they connect cultures and generations. So, let's dive into how cross-cultural families use popular culture to blend traditions and reimagine them in creative ways. This is a chapter about family road trips, Spotify playlists, sports fandom, TV shows and more.

Defining Popular Culture

Popular culture surrounds most of us every day. We listen to music. We watch films. We cheer for our favorite sports teams. We follow fashion trends. We enjoy folk stories. Popular culture is a big part of the world we live in, even if we don't often stop to acknowledge it. It entertains us. It helps us relax. It can also connect us to others who share our interests. For cross-cultural families, popular culture can also help keep connections to a distant culture alive. Reflecting on my own experiences, popular culture offers opportunities to connect with my child and introduce them to other cultures. But what exactly is popular culture, and how does it differ from media?

At its core, popular culture consists of the activities, content, symbols and stories that resonate broadly within society. Raymond Williams famously described culture as 'ordinary' and connected to the lived experiences of people.[1] Popular culture, in this sense, is created and shaped by communities. It includes everything from Bollywood films, like those Amit's children binge-watch, to sports, music and even food.

Unlike media, which I use to refer to technologies or platforms (think YouTube, Disney+ or TikTok), popular culture is about content. As I already mentioned, it is about songs, stories, materials and symbols that engage audiences. Popular culture is neither static nor trivial; it is crucial to how we make sense of the world around us. It is also a space where meanings are contested, affirmed, or reshaped.[2] For instance, Seema's daughter finds pride in her South Asian identity when she watches *Mira, Royal Detective*. She is, in essence, a fan who enjoys the story and makes connections to her own life.[3] The cross-cultural families I met also actively engage with popular culture. They do not just consume content. They use it to interpret, create and connect with the world around them.

Intergenerational Fandom and Popular Culture

Coco, a 2017 animated Disney film about a boy's journey into the Land of the Dead, became more than just a movie in Manuel's Mexican-Swedish-American household. The story, the setting and costumes introduced Mexican culture to his young son. The film also became an intergenerational experience as the whole family (including the grandparents) watched it together. 'My parents introduced *Coco* to my son to keep him rooted in Mexican culture', Manuel shared when I talked with him. He also remembered that the film led them to conversations about *Día de los Muertos* (Day of the Dead) traditions and the role that family plays in Mexican culture. In effect, the film introduced Manuel's son to a culture that might have otherwise felt distant to a small boy growing up in the United States.

I've experienced similar moments with my son. From early on, I made it a point to watch filmed versions of Czech fairy tales with him. Sitting down to watch a classic rendition of *Tři Oříšky pro Popelku* (Three Wishes for Cinderella) allowed me to share the popular culture that my mother had shared with me. Like Manuel's experience with *Coco*, these moments remind me of the powerful role popular culture plays in connecting generations and fostering a deeper understanding of where we come from.

Other parents do the same. Jessica mentioned two major popular culture touchstones when I talked to her about her Irish, Argentinian and American family: the special Christmas edition of *The Late Late Show* and Argentinian football. For Jessica and her husband, enjoying these shows and sports connects them to each other and to their cultural heritage. 'We watch the Irish Late Late Toy Show, and the kids support my husband's football club in Argentina', she shared with me. Watching the *Toy Show*, which features Irish toys and performers, connects her children to their Irish roots in a way that feels tangible and fun, even though they're living in the United States. Cheering on Argentinian football players helps them feel like they are still part of a broader Argentinian community.

Beyond these more nostalgic connections, shared popular culture can also become the starting point for families to build something new together. As I already observed, popular culture isn't just entertainment; it can also be a space where stories, traditions, and values come alive.[4]

Popular Culture as a Cultural Bridge

While introducing children to cultural heritage was a priority for some parents, other parents I interviewed also used popular culture to consciously bridge cultural differences and make sense of their children's multicultural identities. At first glance, the activities and content they engage in look very much the same. They cheer on their favorite sports team. They stream TV shows. They follow YouTube influencers in their home countries. But they do this with the understanding that their goal is to expand their children's cultural repertoire. In Gabriela's Chilean and American home, the family cheers on the Chilean soccer team whenever they play. Even after moving from Chile to Bowling Green, Kentucky, her children's enthusiasm for the national team remains strong, a cultural thread. 'If the Chilean soccer team is playing, they are going to cheer', Gabriela says. She also acknowledges that her children identify strongly as Americans and that they do not see it as an either/or proposition. Supporting Chile in soccer is simply a way for them to express one of their identities.

Alyssa, a third-culture kid (TCK) who grew up in Cameroon and moved to the United States for college, shared a similar experience. In Cameroon, she and her friends bonded over *The Fresh Prince of Bel-Air*. 'The big thing was *Fresh Prince of Bel-Air*... we were always delayed because someone had to go get a CD or tape and bring it back', she explained. For Alyssa and her peers, the show became a shared cultural experience, one that bridged their African and American worlds. The shared joy and humor of *Fresh Prince* allowed them to navigate their TCK identities while bonding over the familiar experiences of teenage life depicted on screen. In other words, popular culture helped Alyssa connect with others.

These experiences with popular culture align with Arjun Appadurai's concept of *mediascapes*, which emphasizes how media circulates cultural symbols and narratives across global contexts.[5] Appadurai argues that these cultural flows allow people to imagine and inhabit shared spaces that transcend physical borders. In the process, popular culture becomes a tool for fostering connections, enabling individuals to experience and negotiate their multiple identities and perspectives.

Take the story Mai and the Disney film *Frozen*. Mai grew up in Vietnam and is now raising her three-year-old daughter in the Netherlands. For her, *Frozen* opened the door for her daughter to connect with her multiple countries. Her daughter first heard about the film from a friend at her daycare, who invited her to role-play as the characters Elsa and Anna. The space the two girls shared connected them to their own friendship and to the one in the film. Then Mai had an idea. She could also use *Frozen* to reinforce her daughter's connection to her Vietnamese heritage. So, she introduced her daughter to the Vietnamese version of the film first. She later showed her the English and the Dutch versions as well.

For the parents I met, popular culture becomes a tool they use to connect what could otherwise be seen as distinct cultural worlds. The figurative and literal language of popular culture allows them to access their heritage but also make it their own.

Fandom and Identity in Cross-Cultural Families

Beyond lessons in cultural heritage, popular culture also provides useful tools for exploring and negotiating identities, especially in cross-cultural contexts. According to Advika, a Bollywood dance teacher based in Los Angeles, parents and their children use Bollywood films and the song-and-dance sequences to playfully engage their Indian (and South Asian) identities without the pressure of 'getting it right'. 'Bollywood dance connects children to Indian culture and music', Advika explains, emphasizing how the vibrant, expressive dance form welcomes open-ended exploration. The dance classes she teaches allow children to engage with the form with an emphasis on blending tradition and contemporary movements. For these children, Bollywood dance serves as a space to explore their hybrid identities, balancing their Indian heritage with their American upbringing, and creating a cultural bridge through fandom (more on that in Chapter 7).

Originally from Iraq, Fatima has found that popular culture is a powerful cultural tool for her children. When her family arrived in the US, she and her siblings quickly realized the importance of 'catching up' on American movies and television to bridge the gap with their peers. Disney classics like *Aladdin* and *Beauty and the Beast* became essential for Fatima, offering her a common language to bond with classmates and integrate into American social circles, while still carrying memories of her Iraqi roots.

Now a mother, Fatima continues to introduce Disney movies to her children. At the same time, Fatima's family maintains a connection to their Iraqi roots through her parents' media choices. Her mother, who didn't learn English, still mostly watches Arabic language television, preserving a direct link to the culture she left behind. Her father, who had been exposed to foreign media in Iraq, enjoys both Arabic and American films and holds a particular fondness for Denzel Washington's movies.

Whether through Bollywood dance, Disney films, sports or other content, fandom offers a way for families to engage with cultural narratives that reflect both their heritage and their contemporary experiences. Popular culture creates a space where identities are actively negotiated, formed, and performed. For cross-cultural families, this process is especially meaningful, as it allows them to blend their cultural heritage with the new environments they inhabit. Through fandom, families find ways to connect across generations and cultures, building a sense of belonging that transcends borders.

Popular Culture and Creative Storytelling

I opened this chapter with Amit and *Ms. Marvel*. While Amit's children use *Ms. Marvel* to connect with their Indian-American cultural identities, the show also creates opportunities for conversations about cultural identity, representation and the blending of their Indian and American influences. Amit recalls, 'It wasn't just about watching the show. It was about talking with them afterward, asking them what they noticed about the cultural cues or how they saw themselves in the story', he shares. In these conversations, stories from the screen spill over into family life, creating opportunities for deeper reflection and creative storytelling.

Popular culture can indeed invite audiences to actively create their own meanings as they engage with content. For families like Amit's, watching a show like *Ms. Marvel* becomes a shared experience where each family member contributes their perspectives, creating a collective narrative that reinforces their cultural identity. As Henry Jenkins reminds us, popular culture fans rework media texts to fit their own lives, making media not just something to watch, but something to engage with on a personal and community level. In Amit's case, the show leads to discussions about representation and belonging.

Sujata's culturally Indian household exemplifies a creative approach to media that fosters a deep sense of cultural connection and self-expression. Central to this is Sujata's creativity. She wrote and illustrated a book of Tamil baby songs. In it, she blended languages and lyrics to make it more than just a book. The book became a resource for her family. Sujata's son's love for music has since blossomed into a personal fusion of Western and Indian influences in his compositions. 'He's very much into music composing, and it's Western music, but when you listen, you can hear the Indian influence', Sujata notes.

Across these stories, a clear theme emerges: cross-cultural families use popular culture not just for entertainment but as a tool for creative engagement and cultural storytelling. From Amit's discussions about representation in *Ms. Marvel* to Sujata's baby songs, families are actively participating in the creation of meaning, shaping how media influences their lives and identities.

A Starting Point

As I think about how popular culture shows up in my cross-cultural parenting, I'm reminded of all the Večerníčeks, the short evening children's show episodes on Czech Television, that I've watched with my son. Enter *Bob a Bobek*, the classic Czech cartoon featuring two mischievous rabbits who live in a magician's hat. In each episode, Bob, the more responsible rabbit, tries to convince his sleep-loving sidekick,

Bobek, to join him on various adventures. Together, they encounter everything from quaint Czech towns to whimsical, far-off places, with each escapade bringing new laughs and lessons.

Watching *Bob a Bobek* is a fun, tangible way to share my own Czech heritage with my son. Like Amit's children, who find a bridge to their South Asian roots in *Ms. Marvel*, my son encounters his Czech identity through these beloved stories. But, our time with *Bob a Bobek* also leads to deeper conversations, particularly when cultural stereotypes show up as they do in the episode where the two rabbits travel to the American West.

These moments provide a chance for us to pause and talk about what these images represent and why they can be problematic. We discuss how portrayals of Native Americans in older media often relied on stereotypes, and I explain that these portrayals don't reflect the full diversity and richness of Native cultures. This conversation is similar to conversations other parents shared. Together, my son and I explore why it's important to question these portrayals and consider the perspectives and histories of the people depicted through them.

As we enjoy and reflect, *Bob a Bobek* helps me connect with my son. The experience brings us closer. We have also used it to create a family tradition that is uniquely our own. So, if I were to share what I've learned with other parents, I would say that you should find those cultural gems that mean something to you and let them become part of your family's story. Popular culture, whether through cartoons, superhero shows or even sports fandom, offers a unique way to connect across cultures and generations.

Notes

(1) Williams, 1958.
(2) Hall, 1997.
(3) Jenkins, 1992.
(4) Jenkins *et al.*, 2013.
(5) Appadurai, 1996.

Takeaways from Chapter 5

Popular culture builds bridges across cultures and generations. Parents can use films, music and sports events to connect their children with their cultural roots.

Shared fandom brings families closer. From cheering for a favorite soccer team to singing along to Bollywood songs, shared popular culture moments can strengthen family connections.

Media representation can lead to meaningful conversations. A series like *Ms. Marvel* or a film like *Coco* opens the door to genuine conversations about identity, representation and what 'home' means.

Popular culture inspires creativity. Letting kids remix songs, reenact scenes or craft fan art invites them to experiment with who they are and where they belong.

Popular culture can help cross-cultural families. More than mere entertainment, popular culture can become a toolkit where heritage and new influences mix and remix.

Reflection Questions – Chapter 5

Here are five reflection questions you might consider based on the themes included in this chapter:

(1) What types of popular culture (like books, music, films or TV shows) are meaningful to you? How have you shared them with your children? What was their reaction?

(2) How has popular culture influenced your child's understanding of their cultural heritage? Can you think of specific movies, shows, songs or books that helped them connect to their identity?

(3) Describe a time when popular culture created a meaningful cultural bond within your family. Was it through a shared viewing experience, a discussion connected to a story or a tradition inspired by a cultural reference?

(4) How do you strike a balance between introducing stories and content from your own cultural background and making room for the popular content your child wants to consume because of where you live? What strategies have helped you maintain this balance?

(5) What challenges have you faced in finding popular culture that accurately represents your child's cross-cultural experiences? Do you try to make sure that the media they watch does bridge cultural gaps and does not reinforce stereotypes or exclusions?

Activity: Cultural Stories Reimagined

Purpose and Benefits

This activity invites participants from different generations to explore how cultural stories and media have evolved over time or across cultures. By comparing media from different periods or cultural contexts, families can reflect on cultural shifts, representation and values. It also provides an opportunity to creatively reimagine these stories, blending traditions with modern influences to highlight shared values and heritage.

Duration: 40–60 minutes (plus media-watching time)

- Watching media: Flexible depending on the selected pieces.
- Discussion and comparison: 20–30 minutes.
- Creative reimagining: 15–20 minutes.

What You Will Need

- Access to two media pieces (e.g. TV shows, films, music videos) from different time periods or cultural backgrounds.
- Pen and paper (optional for taking notes or creative brainstorming).
- Art materials (optional for creative extensions like storyboards or illustrations).
- Synchronous video conferencing platform (optional for virtual participants).

How to Do It

(1) **Watch:**
   - **Older Participant:** Choose a media piece from your childhood or cultural background (e.g. a TV show, film or music video). Watch it together and explain its cultural or personal significance.
   - **Younger Participant:** Choose a contemporary media piece you enjoy that connects to the first one through themes, characters or cultural elements. Watch it together and share why it resonates with you.

(2) **Compare and Reflect:**
   - Discuss the similarities and differences between the two media pieces using prompts like:
     o   How do the two stories represent cultural or social values?
     o   What cultural elements (e.g. language, customs, food, dress) are present, and how do they reflect the time or cultural context?
     o   How are topics like family, community or heroes portrayed differently?
     o   How has technology or storytelling style evolved?
   - Optional: Create a visual representation of these comparisons by listing or drawing key elements of each story.

(3) Create a Cross-Cultural Story:
- Blend elements from both media pieces to create a new story that reflects both time periods and cultural contexts.
- Use these guiding questions:
  - o What elements of each story would you keep? Why?
  - o What would you change or leave out to update the themes?
  - o How could this new story reflect both participants' cultural identities and family heritage?

(4) Optional Extensions:
- **Story Creation**: Create a storyboard or act out a scene from the new story using toys, props or costumes. For example, blend a traditional folktale with a modern superhero narrative.
- **Illustration**: Draw a key moment from the reimagined story, incorporating symbols, colors or elements from both cultural contexts.

Reflection or Follow-Up (Optional)

- How did this activity change your perspective on cultural stories from different generations or backgrounds?
- What did you learn about each other's cultural or personal experiences through the stories you shared?
- How does media reflect or influence your sense of cultural identity?

Part 3
Cross Cultures in Everyday Life

6 Feed the Imagination

Figure 6.1 Shared meals can feed the cross-cultural imagination. (credit A. Desai)

I am a huge fan of *The Great British Bake Off*. I particularly love the earlier seasons because they opened my eyes to the possibilities of cross-cultural baking. Season 3 from 2015 is probably my favorite because it featured several contestants with mixed backgrounds. Nadiya Hussain was one of them. She actually went on to win that season and also achieved a cross-cultural victory along the way. As a Muslim contestant of Bangladeshi origin, she made it clear that food bridges between cultures. Nadiya's (and other contestants') journey through the show wasn't simply about perfecting bake times and icing consistency. In *The Great British Bake Off*, every cross-cultural baked good invited audiences to rethink their assumptions about flavors and textures.

In the finale that season, Nadiya created a stunning lemon drizzle wedding cake. She explained that this 'big fat British wedding cake' was a tribute to the British wedding she never had, as she married in Bangladesh.[1] Decorated with jewels, the cake blended her Bangladeshi heritage with her life in the United Kingdom, inspiring others to do the same. Her victory made the possibilities of blended cultures visible in a hopeful (and dare I say tasty) way. She soon published *Nadiya's Kitchen*, a recipe book which includes many cross-cultural recipes and bounces back and forth between cultures. Bengali Korma is followed by Hazelnut Truffles and photos of her children happy, comfortable and enjoying what she made for them.

Food is a central topic and powerful tool for many cross-cultural parents. Whether it's through family recipes, festive holiday meals or creative modern takes on traditional dishes, food provides a tangible link to cultures and memories. Food is a basic need and a physical experience, making it one of the more accessible tools that parents can use to support their children's explorations of their cross-cultural backgrounds. With its ability to bring up memories and connections, food is almost like a living archive, a medium that helps us share cultural knowledge, stories and values.

In the survey that I fielded, an overwhelming number, namely 87% of respondents, identified food as central to their cross-cultural parenting. So, in this chapter I share what I learned. The bottom line is that we really are what we eat. The culinary choices we make with our children leave a lasting imprint which transcends time and place. Baking together can stir up memories of kneading dough with a grandmother. The warm, earthy scent of cumin might transport us to family celebrations half a world away.

The Family Table: A Classroom for Cultural Traditions

Gabriela, a Chilean mother raising her children in the United States, preserves her family's cultural identity through food. 'I cook every day', she said to me when we talked. 'The cooking and feeding habits are very much our culture'. Cooking Chilean dishes helps Gabriela to ensure that her children remain connected to their roots even as they live somewhere else. To her, each meal she prepares carries with it a piece of her homeland, offering her children a sensory connection to the sights, smells and flavors of Chile. Gabriela's experience reflects a broader commitment I observed in many of the cross-cultural families I met through my study. As food scholars who focus on food and culture highlight, food and shared meals are deeply tied to culture for many people, especially those who need to make a conscious choice to seek out ingredients and recipes that tie to their memories even as they live somewhere else.[2]

To many of the parents I spoke with, the family table serves as a classroom. This is where their children taste the food their parents knew growing up. This is where they hear stories about a place they may only visit. This is where they learn about the traditions and values that their parents associate with these meals. Food transmits cultural knowledge. Each meal becomes a lesson in cultural heritage. Recipes are not merely prepared; they are guides to navigating cultural connections and memories.

In her book *Cuisine and Culture: A History of Food and People*, Linda Civitello (2011) highlights the profound role food has played in shaping human history and cultural expression. She notes that food has always been an integral part of cultural identity, offering people a way to express who they are, where they come from and how they understand the world. For cross-cultural families, food becomes even more important as they navigate the intersection of multiple identities, using food as a tangible connection to their heritage.

For parents, food often provides the most tangible connection to their past. It can also be a commitment. The parents I spoke with told me about how hard it can be to source the right ingredients. They scour the 'world' sections of supermarkets and sometimes drive long distances to access specialty grocery stores. They even make it a point to join local diasporic communities that organize food-focused events around festivals and holidays. This is particularly true for families who worry that distance will weaken their connections to their cultural roots.

For Gabriela and other parents, keeping her country's food front and center on her family's dinner table helps her feel in control of her family's cultural identity. The meals she prepares remind her and her family that they still have some roots in the homeland they left behind. Food gives her a sense of continuity.

Cooking in the Cloud: Exploring Heritage Through Food Media

Food cultures are not just about eating. They are also about media. Amit, an Indian-American father I introduced in Chapter 5, reflects on how his children use food media to connect with their South Asian roots. 'Food is a big part of cross-cultural parenting... and there's a really interesting connection now between food and media', he shared. He then went on to describe how his children turn to Indian-American YouTubers and TikTok creators to learn about Indian cooking. These creators connect Indian cooking to their own cultural background as they break down complex recipes into manageable steps.

From shows like *The Great British Bake Off* to cooking channels on YouTube and TikTok, food focused media is now popular among many cross-cultural families. Did you forget how to make that special dish that your grandmother used to make in the winter? Chances are that there are several versions of the recipe available online. Food media has opened new possibilities to how families engage with their culinary heritage. We might even think about this content as a sprawling resource library, where parents and their children learn how to prepare traditional dishes or discover new ways to incorporate cultural flavors into everyday recipes.

This role for food media is not new by any means. In fact, Arjun Appadurai pointed to how food media fosters cultural connection and inclusivity, breaking down barriers between communities almost four decades ago. In his 1988 essay *How to Make a National Cuisine: Cookbooks in Contemporary India*, Appadurai highlights how pre-digital cookbooks became symbols for cultural and national identity.[3] These ideas resonate even more strongly in digital spaces where food media becomes both about celebrating food traditions and a space where content creators connect with their own lived experiences.

For Amit's children, food is a tangible experience which makes food-related media a productive space for engaging with their own cultural identities. They can connect to the cross-cultural experiences that these content creators share. They may nod along when a content creator describes how it feels to have your lunch smell 'different' because your parents packed you a thermos with chicken curry instead of a sunflower butter and jam sandwich. They may chuckle at the inside joke when people don't understand that calling 'naan' 'naan bread' is like saying 'bread bread'.

When Amit described these experiences to me, I thought back to Nadiya Hussain's journey on *The Great British Bake Off*. Throughout the competition, Nadiya consistently incorporated flavors and techniques from her Bangladeshi heritage into classic British baking. She also always made this connection explicit in the stories she told as she baked. Whether it was adding cardamom to a traditional British sponge cake or drawing on South Asian sweets for inspiration, Nadiya's bakes were about her negotiated identity as a British-Bangladeshi Muslim woman and mother. Her success on the show made food media a platform for cross-cultural storytelling even more visible.

Blending Flavors, Blending Identities: Food as Adaptation and Innovation

Cross-cultural families adapt their menus and palates to fit their current cultural context and ingredient availability. Mai, a Vietnamese mother living in the Netherlands, shared this experience. 'I cook from different countries, so my daughter is very open to trying new dishes', Mai explains. Blending and expanding food choices, helps Mai teach her daughter about both her Vietnamese heritage, her home in the Netherlands and the multicultural world she could one day inhabit. She uses food to invite her daughter to think more expansively about her cross-cultural identity.

Evelyn, whom I introduced in Chapter 2, is originally from Hong Kong. She now lives in the Czech Republic with her family where she had her own experiences when it comes to food. At home, her family's meals reflect both Chinese and Czech influences. She uses her rice cooker almost daily, and it occupies a central place on her kitchen counter where it sits right next to the home-made Czech jams and pickles. Her children's food tastes are similarly eclectic. They like Czech food but tend to embellish their dishes with soy sauce and chilli.

Tammi grew up between the Dominican Republic and the United States. Now a parent herself, she often thinks back on how her father introduced her and her siblings to diverse cuisines to ensure they would be open to cultures different from their own. He even made sure that his family lived in a multicultural neighborhood when they lived in Washington, DC to ensure that his children connected with people from different cultures on a daily basis. All of these experiences planted the seeds that took root and showed up when Tammi became a parent herself. Like her father, she now makes it a point to expose her child to international and multicultural experiences, with food being a key tool in her approach.

The parents I met use food to create shared moments that invite their children to engage with their cross-cultural identities. The kitchen then becomes more of an experiment, a lab, where the old and new are blended and remixed to create fresh, unique tastes that reflect the real lived experiences of cross-cultural families. While they may still hold on to notions of what makes something 'authentic', they may also want to explore how their food experiences evolve and change. These lived experiences resonate with the work of scholars who find that migration leads to the transformation of food practices. As people travel and resettle their palates change. They then seek out food experiences that reflect their own hybrid identities. They want their flavors to reflect who they have become.[4]

Beyond the family kitchen, food festivals, online videos and digital tutorials further enrich these explorations, making diverse culinary traditions more accessible. Fusion cuisine is one of the most visible ways cross-cultural families express their culinary creativity, directly reflecting their hybrid identities. This style of cooking, which combines elements from different culinary traditions, has gained global popularity, and many cross-cultural families use it to celebrate both tradition and innovation in their kitchens.

Food-focused gatherings also allow cross-cultural families to experience food as a communal, celebratory practice. Isabela, a Greek mother raising her children in a multicultural household, often invites friends to share Greek traditions over dinner. 'Even when I don't have a Greek community nearby, I try to create that sense of connection by sharing our dishes and traditions with friends who are curious and eager to learn', she explains. These gatherings immerse her family in Greek culture and help them connect with others who are experiencing similar diasporic and cross-cultural realities. Food helps them celebrate the diverse cultural influences that shape their lives.

So, food is both a window to the past and a bridge to the future. Food can help us honor our cultural roots. It can also become a space where we and our children negotiate their own cross-cultural experiences. We may even use food to push past our experiences to learn about palates and cultures beyond our own.[5]

From Koláče to Curry

As I stand in my kitchen in Los Angeles, my hands dusted with flour, the smell of freshly baked *koláče* (traditional pastries) fills the air. I am using a recipe my grandmother passed down to me, one she had perfected in her kitchen in rural Czech Republic. The *koláče* I bake for my son are more than just pastries. Each ball of dough topped with poppy seeds and farmer's cheese helps me feel connected to my own grandmother and everything she stood for in my life. As Marek takes a bite of the sweet, pillowy dough filled with poppy seed filling, I almost feel like my grandmother is there with me, smiling at him, at us. I can almost believe we are all in her kitchen in the Czech village where I spent my summers as a child. Almost. For Marek and I, *koláče* become more than just a treat; they connect us to a past that shaped our family's story for generations.

And yet, my son is not just Czech. He is a blend of cultures, as many cross-cultural children are. His heritage stretches beyond the Czech Republic, traveling across continents to South Asia. There, Indian spices call to him through a dish he loves: chicken curry. When he takes a bite of chicken curry that his Indian grandmother makes for him, he gets an expression that can only be described as pure bliss. Looking at him, I imagine that he is being transported to India, a place where he can explore the other half of his identity, despite the fact that he has not been there yet. Through chicken curry and rice, he connects to the stories, flavors and traditions of his South Asian roots. He can also love *koláče* and the memories of his Czech great-grandmother.

So, our experience with food is defined by *koláče* just as much as by chicken curry. Food becomes the bridge between two worlds that may seem far away but are brought together through the act of preparing and sharing meals. Like Mai, we also make it a point to expose Marek to other cuisines and take advantage of the diverse restaurant offerings we have all around us. As I write this, we have just returned from a meal at our favorite Thai restaurant.

For Marek, all these meals and dishes are more than just food. They are imagined journeys and experiences that invite him to connect to his family's past and to explore his current life in the United States. As a parent, I see the power that these culinary experiences hold. They offer him not just nourishment but a sense of belonging to both sides of his heritage. When he enjoys *koláče*, he is connected to the land and family of his Czech ancestry; when he enjoys curry, he is exploring the rich heritage of his South Asian roots. When he explores other cuisines, he learns about new flavors and becomes open to more cuisines. In these moments, food serves as a cultural compass, guiding him as he explores the many dimensions of his identity.

Our story is not unique. Many parents I met shared that food helps them connect their families to their heritage. Through food, they offered their children a way to experience their cultural background, even when it was hard to actually visit. Parents also used food to explore their cross-cultural experiences. They encouraged their children to try new foods and mix ingredients to create new combinations and flavors. Food in cross-cultural families is all about creativity and adaptation. Food for us is about blending flavors and traditions so that our children feel connected to all aspects of who they are.

Notes

(1) Ward & Singh, 2015.
(2) Counihan & Julier, 2017.
(3) Appadurai, 1988.
(4) Ray & Srinivas, 2012.
(5) Crowther, 2013.

Takeaways from Chapter 6

Food carries family stories forward. Parents turn recipes into living records, using meals to share memories and customs across generations and cultures.

The kitchen is a space for tradition AND creativity. Daily cooking and mealtime rituals become lessons in where you come from and a chance to invent new traditions together.

Food media brings cross-cultural culinary experiences into the digital era. Platforms like YouTube and TikTok are informal classrooms where families can explore classic recipes and experiment with new takes on tradition.

Mixing flavors reflects blending identities. Trying out fusion dishes and unexpected ingredients lets families celebrate the rich, layered nature of their cross-cultural lives.

Meals feed both appetite and curiosity. Sharing a meal invites stories of the places and people behind the flavors.

Reflection Questions – Chapter 6

Here are five reflection questions you might consider based on the themes included in this chapter:

(1) Are there recipes in your family that mean a lot to you or have a story behind them? Have you been able to share these with your kids?

(2) How have user-generated content platforms like YouTube, Instagram or TikTok helped your family when it comes to cooking and celebrating food? Have they helped preserve traditional dishes or encouraged you to experiment?

(3) Think about a time when you shared a meal with someone from a different cultural background. Did that experience help you get to know them better?

(4) How do you navigate blending multiple culinary influences in the kitchen?

(5) How can cooking or sharing culturally specific meals help children connect with their cultural roots? How does incorporating food-related traditions into a family reinforce such connections?

Activity: Whisking Up Stories

Purpose and Benefits

This activity creates a space for cross-cultural parents and children to share stories about food, culture and family traditions. Through storytelling and an optional cooking activity, it fosters connection, cultural appreciation and creativity.

Duration: 45–60 minutes

- Introduction and setup: 5–10 minutes.
- Sharing stories: 30–40 minutes (depending on group size).
- Optional cooking or reflection: 10–15 minutes.

What You Will Need

- An ingredient or cooking tool (e.g. a spice, vegetable or special kitchen utensil) meaningful to your culture.
- Paper and writing tools for jotting down notes or thoughts.
- A comfortable space arranged in a circle or around a table for sharing.
- Optional: Kitchen setup with basic cooking equipment and ingredients if planning to cook.

How to Do It

(1) Bring an Ingredient or Cooking Tool:
- Each participant (parent and child) brings:
  - o An ingredient with cultural significance (e.g. a spice, vegetable or grain); or
  - o A cooking tool they use often or that holds cultural meaning (e.g. a rolling pin, family recipe book).

(2) Share Your Story:
- Gather in a circle or around a table. Take turns sharing:
  - o Why you chose this ingredient or tool.
  - o What meal or dish you would make with it.
  - o Any family or cultural significance it holds.
  - o A story or memory connected to using it.

(3) Who Would You Invite?
- Imagine who you'd invite to enjoy this meal:
  - o This could be a family member, friend or historical/cultural figure.
- Share why you'd invite them and what it would mean to share this meal together.

(4) Optional: Cook Together:
- If inspired and time allows, collaborate to cook using the ingredients or ideas shared.

- Cooking is optional. The main focus is on storytelling and connecting through food.

(5) **Reflect and Enjoy:**
- Reflect on the different cultural connections shared.
- Use discussion prompts like:
  - o How did hearing others' stories broaden your understanding of their culture or your own?

Reflection or Follow-Up (Optional)

- How did this activity help you appreciate cultural diversity within your family or group?
- Are there other dishes or tools you'd like to explore together in the future?

7 Sing and Dance

Figure 7.1 Cross-cultural parents may turn to a little song-and-dance.
(credit A. Desai)

Rohit is in his early twenties and lives in North Carolina. He loves Bollywood dance and credits it with helping him come to terms with his Indian-American identity. He discovered his love for Bollywood dance in a somewhat unexpected place: the empty rooms of the motel his parents operated. It was here that Rohit, then 11 years old, would plug in a pair of old Dell speakers, turn up the Bollywood music and just dance. 'I pretty much went on YouTube and started watching other dancers and videos of dance performances, dance teams, dance crews, so on and so forth. I watched all that stuff... I started dancing in an empty motel room', Rohit recalls.

Rohit's introduction to Bollywood dance was largely self-driven. He sought out content online. He looked for Hindi film clips featuring dance. He also kept an eye out for filmed dances that dancers around the world had uploaded to various platforms, mostly YouTube. Using these videos as guides, he experimented with movements and expressions that caught his attention. If he couldn't do something, he kept trying or found an alternative that worked for him. Over time, Bollywood dance became something he really enjoyed and something that connected him to his Indian heritage. Once his parents found out about his interest in dance, they supported him. His first live performance took place at his cousin's wedding, where he put his self-taught skills on display for an audience of friends and relatives. The performance was a success, marking the beginning of Rohit's more public engagement with Bollywood dance.

Unlike Rohit, children enrolled in Nakul Dev Mahajan Studios (NDM) dance classes learn Bollywood dance in a live studio setting. Founded in 1998 and based in Cerritos, NDM is one of Los Angeles's oldest and largest Bollywood-focused dance schools. Over the years, it has served thousands of students, offering them a shared space to connect with Indian culture. Recitals highlight the collaborative and celebratory nature of the studio. I attended one of these recitals on 8 November 2023. The recital was called 'Shaadi' (Wedding) and filled with the sights, sounds and aromas that I associate with Indian festivals. There were samosas for sale in the lobby and the vast majority of the student performers and audience members seemed to be of South Asian origin. They performed choreographed dances that blended humor, storytelling and a heavy dose of Indian nostalgia. Dances in the show were performed by student dancers dressed in sequined Indian gowns, shimmering bangles and intricate jewelry. All these elements signaled that this was an event about shared heritage on display.

In thinking about Bollywood dance and cross-cultural parenting, I was first struck by the stark contrast between Rohit and the dancers at NDM. Rohit learned Bollywood dance by watching and emulating online videos. The students at NDM take classes in person and perform at events that draw a supportive, culturally connected audience. And yet, these two experiences do have something in common. They are both centrally about physically experienced performance. Whether in a solitary motel room or a bustling recital hall, song-and-dance becomes a medium for navigating and embodying cultural identity.

Why Focus on Song-and-Dance?

I realize it may seem strange that I chose to dedicate so much space to song-and-dance in a book about media, but that is precisely the point. We often think about media as a disembodied practice that is detached from physical experience. Yet media can engage our bodies deeply, as it does through dance and music. And these media allow children and parents to experience their heritage physically. For parents navigating cross-cultural parenting, song-and-dance offer a unique way to connect children with their heritage. Whether through formal Bollywood dance classes like those at NDM or self-directed exploration like Rohit's, these practices create spaces where children can physically experience and express their identities.

In this chapter, I invite you to think about the physical experiences of raising cross-cultural children. The focus here is not on pursuing music or dance as a career or achieving mastery. Whether solitary or communal, formal or playful, these experiences highlight how physical experiences can create meaningful connections. Far from being in opposition to digital experiences, these physical activities often intertwine with online modes of learning and expression.

Why Bollywood?

Why include a case study on Bollywood in a book about cross-cultural parenting? The answer lies in its extraordinary ability to bridge divides, not only between generations but also between countries. Bollywood, an eclectic dance style inspired by the song-and-dance sequences contained in Hindi films, is uniquely positioned as a visible and widely accessible cultural practice. Known for its catchiness, Bollywood is welcoming and open to interpretation. For families with ties to South Asia, it can also become a tool that helps them maintain their heritage.[1] But its value extends far beyond its origins.

For parents who may not share ties to Indian or South Asian cultures, Bollywood offers a rich example of how music and dance can help children navigate hybrid identities.[2] Bollywood dance exemplifies how physical and expressive activities can become vehicles for exploring and embodying heritage in ways that are both joyful and deeply meaningful. Some parents may enroll their children in formal classes. Others may rely on family to transmit music and dance traditions. Still others may choose to turn to the internet and user-generated video content for inspiration. Bollywood dance is a globally visible dance genre that is also very flexible and adaptable. In other words, Bollywood dance can mean many things to many people.

I have personally experienced Bollywood dance in this way. Growing up between cultures, I often felt a sense of outsider status, caught between my Czech and Nepali heritage. Bollywood dance became a way for me to reconcile these fragmented identities. Watching Hindi film songs at my cousin's video rental store in Kathmandu, I found a mirror for my own struggles. The fearless blending of traditions I saw in Bollywood dance modeled hybrid identity, where different parts of me could coexist. This connection to Bollywood dance ultimately led me to study various dance forms, from Bharatanatyam in Chennai to modern dance at Princeton University. Each experience reinforced that dance is not only a link to heritage but also a way to reimagine and reshape identity.

Now, as a parent, I use music and dance to help my son navigate his own hybrid identity, sharing songs and dances from both his South Asian and Central European roots. At this point, it is clear that platforms like YouTube have made it easier to access content, allowing children like Rohit to engage with their heritage even in the absence of local resources. For families attending studios like NDM, media also serves as a bridge, connecting them to iconic Bollywood songs and performances that evoke collective memories.

So, while this chapter focuses on Bollywood and the South Asian cultural context, the lessons here are more broadly applicable to cross-cultural parenting. I invite you to look to your own cultural or ethnic traditions and find ways to foster physical engagement with heritage through music, dance and performance. Many cultures (Mexico, Brazil, Japan, China, Russia and Afghanistan to name a few) have rich music and dance traditions that offer abundant opportunities for families to connect across generations. Folk dance groups, festival celebrations involving performance, theatrical productions and musical events are just a few examples of how cultures across the world create spaces for embodied cultural practice.

I urge you to think about ways that you can engage with these traditions and adapt them, making them relevant to your cross-cultural realities. Maybe it begins with the Brazilian samba, celebrating Mexico's folklórico traditions, or participating in Chinese New Year lion dances. Maybe it then moves on to a more creative engagement with these traditions. Bollywood dance may be the case study I discuss here, but the hope is really that it will inspire you to explore the music and dance traditions that resonate with you and your families.

Taking Lessons in Indianness (or other cultural heritage)

NDM is one of many Bollywood-focused dance schools in Los Angeles. Bollywood dance-focused schools immerse students in 'Indianness' through music, movement, and dance. As they learn dances, students are invited to connect with a sense of heritage that transcends the physical distance between Los Angeles and India. Beyond this, the schools do try to vary their approach as the instructors choose to focus on different aspects of Bollywood dance to differentiate themselves and their students. Ayana and Advika each run their own Bollywood dance schools and shared with me their insights about why they do this and what they have learned about their students. They both see their studios as spaces that invite students to learn more about Indian culture. Beyond this, they both stress that they bring their own understanding of Bollywood to their dance instruction.

Ayana focuses on storytelling and teaching about cultural heritage. She sees Bollywood dance as media that helps her students get exposed to Indian folklore and Hindi language. In her classes, she incorporates storytelling techniques and introduces Hindi phrases to help students understand the cultural context behind each song. Taking a different approach, Advika highlights Bollywood dance as an adaptable and versatile dance genre. She mixes dance styles into the choreography she creates for the Bollywood songs she teaches and aims to create a welcoming space for her students, no matter what their background. She wants Bollywood dance to celebrate a blending of identities and wants everyone to connect with Indian culture.

Though they differ in their emphasis, Ayana and Advika both immerse their students in a rigorous understanding Bollywood dance as a flexible form that they adapt to their students' cultural needs. This understanding of Bollywood dance as open to interpretation is what makes this dance form uniquely suited for cross-cultural parenting. It is also what makes it very different from more classical Indian dance forms like Bharatanatyam. In sharp contrast to the more playful and accommodating approaches that Bollywood dance teachers take, Indian classical dance school instructors tend to emphasize rigorous discipline, technique, spirituality and tradition. Families who choose to enroll their children in Indian classical dance are making a conscious decision to immerse their children in a rigorous understanding of Indian traditions and values. Though there is some variation between schools, Indian classical dance requires dedication to structured forms, spiritual narratives and symbolism. Such training gives students an understanding of Indian culture that is constant and enduring.

In contrast, Bollywood dance provides a much more easy-going and relaxed introduction to Indian cultures. The form itself blends traditional Indian styles with Western influences, making it even more appealing to parents and students navigating their cross-cultural identities. 'Bollywood dance lets students find joy in their heritage in a way that feels relevant to their daily lives in Los Angeles', Advika explained when I talked with her. She wants Bollywood dance to bridge generations and identities, reflecting both what is passed down and what needs to change.

When parents choose whether they want to enroll their children in Bollywood dance or in Indian classical dance classes, they are in effect deciding how they want to approach their children's physical connection to 'Indianness'. Some families I spoke with over the years feel that Indian classical dance, with its emphasis on tradition, leads to a deeper immersion in Indian culture. Ayana acknowledges this may be true but notes that the rigor of the dance style may not fit a family's lifestyle or priorities. 'Classical dance is beautiful and full of meaning, but it requires a lot of time and discipline', she says. For families navigating multiple cultural influences or for children new to Indian culture, Bollywood offers a more flexible, relatable entry point.

Bollywood's flexibility also makes it accessible to families with diverse backgrounds. Bollywood allows parents and children to engage in a way that feels natural and inviting, rather than something rigid or difficult to understand. Ayana sees Bollywood's cultural adaptability as part of its charm, saying, 'Bollywood is a space where kids can feel proud of their culture, but it's open. It welcomes anyone who wants to join and enjoy it'. This flexibility allows Bollywood dance to become a shared experience for parents and their children.

From what I have seen, Bollywood dance schools outside India can be powerful spaces for cultural negotiation for cross-cultural families. The schools bring together children from Indian and non-Indian backgrounds to learn, perform and connect with Indian culture AND each other. Along the way, the students learn more than choreography. They explore their own identities. They discover how they can think across and through cultures. In the hands of instructors like Advika and Ayana, Bollywood dance classes become lessons in Indianness, inclusivity and cultural exchange.

Digital Media and Physical Expression

Bollywood dance has long been shaped by its hybrid content and tendency to incorporate different dance genres. The rise of digital media exponentially increased Bollywood's reach and ushered in a new era of global circulation for the dances contained in the films and those created by fan dancers. Platforms like YouTube now make it possible for anyone with an internet connection to watch and learn Bollywood dance. This transformation has turned Bollywood dance into an accessible resource for cross-cultural engagement, particularly for children and teens who may not have access to formal instruction but are eager to explore their cultural identity through movement.

YouTube and other user-generated video platforms became a dance studio for Rohit. He was able to access film content through them. He was also able to learn from other dancers who uploaded their choreography to the sites. He watched these videos again and again. He tried to emulate them and build on them. Eventually, he was able to learn the steps, rhythms and styles that define Bollywood dance. Rohit's experience is not unique. Many children and teens, particularly those from diasporic communities, now turn to digital platforms to explore Bollywood dance (and other dance styles) to connect with their heritage and express themselves. When attending dance classes is not possible, YouTube (and other platforms) can step in to become a vital resource that allows young people to engage with their cultural identities on their own terms.

The accessibility of YouTube, TikTok and other platforms also means that Bollywood dance has become even more participatory.

Children and teens from all over the world can learn at their own pace, in their own spaces and share their progress with others through social media. This has created a global, online community of Bollywood dance enthusiasts who connect through shared passion and practice, even if they've never met in person. As Rohit's story demonstrates, these platforms enable young people to take ownership of their cultural expression, developing their dance skills and connecting with others who share their interests.

Nowhere is the impact of Bollywood's global circulation and digital media platforms more evident than in the thriving scene of competitive Bollywood dance teams in US high schools and on college campuses. These teams, composed largely of young second-generation Indian-Americans, have emerged as vibrant spaces for cultural negotiation. The teams become hubs of cultural activity, where students come together not only to practice but also connect with each other. For many second-generation Indian-Americans, joining a Bollywood dance team leads to new friendships with peers who share similar experiences. The competitive nature of these teams also adds another layer of engagement, as students push themselves to perfect their choreography and execution, learning valuable skills in teamwork, leadership and creative expression. Notably, even these teams often rely on social media platforms for choreography, costumes and even tutorials on creating complex dance routines.

Teams serve as spaces where students can explore and express the complexities of their cultural identities. Some teams have used their performances to address issues of intergenerational conflict, particularly around topics such as LGBTQ+ identity. A case in point is that the Bollywood dance team Anubhav from Northwestern University once choreographed a performance that told the story of a young man coming to terms with his homosexuality. The performance touched on themes of family expectations, identity and acceptance. It also challenged traditional norms within Indian culture by creating an inclusive and progressive narrative within the community.

Dance and Song as Tools for Cross-Cultural Parenting

Across many cultures, songs and dances provide direct, physical connections to one's heritage. Whether your child learns Brazilian samba, Greek folk dance or Taiko drumming, they will experience the rhythms, gestures and stories of these cultural practices within their bodies. Whether through song lyrics, the traditional styles incorporated into the movement or the visual and symbolic motifs used in performances, studying culturally specific music and dance traditions can help children connect to their parents' past. This is why many parents seek out these opportunities for their children.

That said, it is also important to ask yourself questions about what this experience will give your child. Is the primary purpose about maintaining a (perhaps nostalgic) connection to another place and culture? Or do you want to use music and dance to help your children express their cross-cultural and hybrid identities? The answer will depend on who you are and what you want for your family.

For some families, cultural dance and music help them hold onto the past. This is often true for parents who cannot travel frequently to their home country and for whom cultural gatherings may be a rare opportunity to share these traditions. In such cases, children can 'remember' and carry forward traditions, even if they've never lived in the places their families originated from. Other parents turn to song-and-dance to open up exploration and dialogue across generations and geographies. Here children also consider their own relationship to their parents' heritage as studying song-and-dance invites them to express both their inherited cultural traditions and their contemporary, cross-cultural experiences.

In Seema's experience, Bollywood dance introduces students to Indian culture, even for children raised far from South Asia. She notes that Bollywood's blend of traditional Indian and Western dance styles mirrors the diasporic experience, providing an enjoyable way for children to connect with their heritage in a familiar cultural format. A parent herself, Seema responded by creating Bollywood-inspired dance classes conducted in simple Hindi. She did this because she recognized that children may not encounter Hindi frequently in their day-to-day lives, so by learning dance in Hindi, they engage with language and culture in a way that feels relevant and enjoyable. This connection is important because it allows her students to access culture without feeling overwhelmed by formal language lessons (more on this playful approach to language learning in Chapter 8).

For these children, particularly those from multiracial and multicultural families, dance is not just about remembering the past; it is also about negotiating their present-day cross-cultural lives. Dance gives children a chance to explore what it means to be both Korean and American, Nigerian and British or a blend of other cultural identities. The integration of contemporary, global influences into traditional forms resonates with their daily lives and surroundings. Dance and music allow them to celebrate their heritage and embrace their multicultural realities.

Embrace the Physical Experience, Even Online

In cross-cultural parenting, creating spaces where children can physically engage with their heritage is essential. Exposing them to various musical and movement genres allows them to connect to culture in ways that words or abstract lessons cannot. We may enroll them in formal classes. We may make it a point to attend community events and gatherings. We just simply invite them to watch and dance along to our favorite music and dance videos. In doing so, we give our children tools that will help them physically reconcile their cross-cultural identities.

What does this talk about Bollywood dance mean for parents who may not share ties to South Asia? I believe the lessons I have shared here extend beyond any one culture. I invite you to think of Bollywood as a case study of how music and dance can support your children. For those of us raising children in cross-cultural or multicultural environments, the key takeaway is this: we can find embodied ways to explore cultural heritage. We can also frame these experiences in ways that help our children navigate their own cross-cultural identities. Dance and music can become sites of both preservation and innovation. We don't have to just replicate the past.

I do have one final thought to share with parents whose families have no obvious ties to embodied cultural traditions. I really do hope that this chapter will remind us all of the near universal nature of music and dance. By introducing our children to music and dance from various cultures, we encourage curiosity, creativity and empathy. Whether through learning a traditional dance, attending multicultural festivals and concerts or even improvising movements at home, these experiences are entry points into culture, identity and the richness of cross-cultural experiences. And, that just may just be more than enough.

Notes

(1) Kao, 2008; Rozario, 2008.
(2) Shresthova, 2011.

Takeaways from Chapter 7

Dance and music bring culture to life. Parents invite their children to learn songs and steps so they can feel traditions, not just hear them.

Traditions grow in new settings. Mixing classic rhythms with more contemporary music genres gives families a chance to create dance experiences that reflect both past and present.

Moving together builds confidence and connection. Whether in a formal class or a living-room dance-off, stepping to the music helps kids stand a little taller and deepens their bond with you.

Online platforms open doors for every household. With YouTube and similar sites, families can explore cultural dances from anywhere, even when local classes aren't available.

Sharing rhythms creates lasting memories. Dancing side by side, singing along and improvising together turns ordinary moments into joyful traditions that unite generations.

Reflection Questions – Chapter 7

Here are five reflection questions you might consider based on the themes included in this chapter:

(1) What music or dances do you enjoy with your kids? Are they tied to a particular culture or tradition?

(2) How do your kids respond to music or dance? Do they have a favorite song or dance that they like a lot? Have they gravitated toward certain styles or cultural influences? How did that happen?

(3) Do your children ever blend different cultural influences when it comes to music and dance? How do they do it?

(4) Think of a meaningful family memory that involves music or dance. Is it connected to a specific celebration, moment or a cultural tradition?

(5) Do you use media (YouTube, streaming services, etc.) to introduce new music and dance styles to your children? How might you branch out to experiment a little more?

Activity: Let's Sing and Dance

Purpose and Benefits

This activity encourages children and parents to engage with music and movement in a way that fosters creativity, emotional expression and cultural exploration. By interpreting music and creating their own dance, families can blend cultural identities and deepen their connection to the art forms they explore.

Duration: 30–45 minutes

- Listening and moving: 15–20 minutes.
- Watching and creating: 15–20 minutes.
- Reflection: 5–10 minutes.

What You Will Need

- Access to YouTube (or another platform) to find music and dance videos.
- Space to move (e.g. living room, backyard, etc.).
- A journal or notepad (optional for reflections or drawings).

How to Do It

(1) **Listen to the Music:**
- **Pick a Song:** Choose a song from a different culture or genre (e.g. Bollywood, classical Indian, folk or a genre you're curious about).
- **Close Your Eyes and Listen:**
  o Focus on how the music makes you feel.
  o Ask questions like:
    ▪ What emotions does the music evoke?
    ▪ Does it remind you of a place or memory?
    ▪ What story might this music be telling?
  o Share your thoughts with each other.

(2) **Move to the Music:**
- **Start Free Movement:** Move to the music without watching any videos.
- Explore how your body naturally responds to the rhythm and sounds.
- Take turns showing movements or try a 'follow the leader' style.

(3) **Watch the Dance Version:**
- **Watch a Video:** Find and watch a dance version of the song (e.g. Bollywood, folk or modern).
- Reflect on how the dancers interpret the music. Discuss:
  o How do their movements differ from or align with yours?
  o What gestures or techniques stood out to you?

(4) Create Your Own Movement:
- **Combine and Create**: Blend the movements you felt in Step 2 with ideas from the dance video.
- Adapt the choreography to make it your own, adding spins, influences from other styles, or playful improvisations.
- Take turns leading new moves or collaborate as a family.

(5) Reflect and Share:
- Discuss the experience:
  - o How did it feel to move to the music before seeing the official dance?
  - o Did watching the dance change your perspective on the song?
  - o How did creating your own movements deepen your connection to the music and each other?
- Optional: Capture the experience through drawings, writing or a creative reflection.

Reflection or Follow-Up (Optional)

- How can you use music and dance as a way to connect with other cultures or traditions?
- What other songs or dances would you like to explore as a family?

8 Play With Languages

Figure 8.1 Scrabble can be played in multiple languages at once! (credit A. Desai)

I was six months pregnant and sitting at my kitchen table when it suddenly hit me: my as-yet-unborn child might never be able to speak to his Czech relatives if I didn't teach him Czech. He would also never appreciate the Nepali culture I grew up with as a child if I didn't share it with him. I was struck by a sense of loss so intense that I didn't know what to do. If my child didn't speak, or at least understand, these languages, how could he fully understand our shared past? How would he grasp who we have become? The full weight of the challenge before me in raising a cross-cultural child suddenly landed on my shoulders. I was completely overwhelmed.

That evening, I raised this concern with my husband. While he supported me then, and continues to do so, we both realized there was no way to do it all. Choices had to be made. In the years that followed, I saw many parents around me grapple with the same challenge. In many ways this is the ultimate challenge of cross-cultural parenting: language. As one wise (and slightly older) parent observed, 'Language is the first thing to go', leaving me with the realization that, for many of us, language feels like an all-or-nothing proposition. And when we fail to achieve full fluency, we often feel like we've failed entirely.

In this chapter, I take a different approach. I borrow from concepts like *translanguaging*, which see language as fluid rather than confined to strict boundaries, to argue that a more flexible approach may open up new linguistic possibilities for cross-cultural families.[1] But I'm getting ahead of myself.

Czechoslovakia's first president Tomáš Garrigue Masaryk is believed to have said, 'Kolik jazyků umíš, tolikrát jsi člověkem', which translates to, 'As many languages you know, so many times you are a person.' This profound statement speaks to the transformative power of language in shaping our identities and understanding of the world. A Persian proverb reinforces this idea with its simple yet evocative wisdom: 'A new language is a new life', reminding us that each language we learn opens up a fresh perspective and a new way of experiencing the world. Similarly, a Turkish saying declares, 'One who speaks only one language is one person, but one who speaks two languages is two people'. Together, these sayings capture the essence of why languages matter.

Language is indeed a gateway to culture, and for cross-cultural parents, it can be one of the most enriching aspects of raising children. But what does it truly mean to know a language? Is it about achieving perfect fluency, or is the answer more complicated? In this chapter, I explore language through the lens of a more playful and flexible world of multilingualism within the family, challenging the conventional focus on flawless bilingualism. Instead, I embrace the natural fluidity of language acquisition and the joy that comes from the unique linguistic blends that can emerge in multicultural homes.

First, Some Context

Growing up in Nepal, it was common for people around me to speak at least three languages. Nepali served as the national language. English was seen as the language we all had to learn to be successful. Many Nepali people also speak their community or ethnic group's language. My husband had a similar experience growing up in India, where he moved between Marathi, Hindi, Gujarati and English. Marathi was the language of his home state. Hindi was the lingua franca of the nation. Gujarati connected him to extended family. English dominated his educational spaces. Moving from language to language was a natural part of daily life for both of us as we grew up.

In fact, multilingualism has historically been a hallmark of many societies. However, in the 19th and 20th centuries, languages became increasingly tied to national and ethnic priorities. Colonial legacies, globalization and nation-building efforts often elevated a single language as a unifying force, sometimes at the expense of others. In Nepal, policies favored Nepali as the sole national language, suppressing indigenous languages despite the country's vast linguistic diversity. Bhim Lal Gautam's research highlights how Nepali and English have been privileged in education and governance, leaving many indigenous languages marginalized.[2]

Nepal is not unusual in taking this approach. In other contexts, such as 19th-century France, regional languages like Breton and Occitan were suppressed to promote French as the sole national language.[3] Similarly, early 20th-century US policies emphasized English-only education to assimilate immigrants, sidelining heritage languages.[4] While these policies often devalued minority languages, shifts in the late 20th and early 21st centuries started to point to the benefits of bilingualism even as discussions around language and national identity rage on in many geographies.[5]

That said, some countries have embraced multilingualism as a cornerstone of their identity. Canada's Official Languages Act (1969) formalized bilingualism in English and French, supported by immersion programs in schools.[6] Switzerland recognizes four national languages, integrating linguistic diversity into its education system from an early age.[7] India's 'Three-Language Formula' aimed to balance regional, national and international language needs but has faced uneven implementation.[8]

I touch on these historical and geopolitical contexts to highlight that multilingualism is more than just a personal or familial choice. It is also deeply influenced by broader societal forces. While this chapter focuses on the intimate, everyday experiences of families navigating multiple languages, it is essential to acknowledge these larger frameworks as they have an effect on parents' experiences with language. We need to recognize that they shape the environments in which families operate, influencing access to resources, and the societal attitudes toward multilingualism.

Bringing Joy: Approaches to Supporting Multilingualism at Home

Raising multilingual children is as much about connection as it is about strategy. Let me explain. The parents I spoke with emphasized that multilingualism within a family unlocks a treasure trove of cognitive, cultural and social benefits, helping children develop a deep sense of identity and belonging. Ultimately, multilingualism is not just about fluency, but also about creating a bridge between heritage and the wider world.

Sujata reflected on the role of language and culture in her children's lives when I spoke to her. She captured her experiences quite eloquently: 'I feel like culture is the best gift that I can give to my children. And language is a gift. Culture is an anchor that helps you stay grounded with a sense of who you belong to, where you come from, and what community you are a part of. It's something you can call your own and share with others'. For Sujata, language and culture are inseparable, connecting her children to traditions, values and rituals they can carry forward throughout their lives.

This connection between language and culture is supported by various well-established approaches to multilingualism. One of the most widely recognized strategies is the One Parent One Language (OPOL) approach, where each parent consistently speaks a different language to the child. This method provides clear boundaries, helping children distinguish between languages and develop proficiency in both.[9] Another approach, Minority Language at Home (mL@H), involves speaking a minority language at home while the majority language is learned in the broader community.[10] Meanwhile, the Time and Place (T&P) approach designates specific times or settings for using different languages, allowing families to integrate multiple languages naturally into their routines.[11]

Of the parents I met, many started with the intention of adhering to a strict approach to language use, such as the OPOL method, but found themselves naturally blending or switching languages depending on the situation. This flexibility, often referred to as *translanguaging*, introduces a more fluid way of navigating multilingual parenting.[12] For Benjamin, whose son speaks a mix of Nepali, English and German, this approach was what worked for his family. 'If he doesn't know the right word, he mixes it with English or German altogether', Benjamin shared. 'It's probably a special language no one else would understand, but it's natural for our family'.

This practice is not only practical but can also be enriching. Daria, an Iranian-American mother, embraces this perspective with her son, Namar. 'It's good enough, right?' she reflected. 'I try to show Namar that there are so many stories in other languages and other countries that he'll never be able to hear if he only knows English'. For many multilingual families, blending languages becomes less about strict adherence to rules and more about creating meaningful ways to connect and communicate.

Of course, *translanguaging* can lead to trade-offs around fluency, and maintaining multiple languages can be hard. Many parents I interviewed described the challenges of maintaining consistency while balancing the demands of daily life. Only 18% of parents surveyed indicated that their children took formal language classes, suggesting that many families rely on informal methods like storytelling, songs and play to keep languages alive. To navigate these challenges, some parents adopt what I call a 'stovetop approach' to languages. Just as you can't pay attention to all burners at once, some languages might require focused effort while others simmer on low.

I am sure language purists and linguists will bristle, but the parents I interviewed taught me that multilingualism isn't about perfection. It's about connection. Whether through stories told in a heritage language, meals shared with grandparents over video calls or playful language blending during family conversations, these moments create a rich, cultural experience.

Languages By Any Media

Digital tools and platforms, from language-learning apps to movies and streaming services, allow parents to bring multiple languages into everyday life, even when formal classes are unavailable or impractical. While maintaining a multilingual household can be challenging, these media resources help children develop linguistic skills and deepen their cultural connections. My survey highlights the growing importance of media in supporting multilingualism. While 62% of the parents I reached reported maintaining multiple languages in the home as key to fostering cultural connection, many also relied on media as a critical tool. For example, 51% of respondents used the internet to access films from different cultures, and 35% engaged with culturally diverse comic books, graphic novels or bilingual books. These numbers reflect how media, in all its forms, complements direct communication within the family.

Marisol, who worked as an ESL instructional assistant, underscores the transformative role of reading in preserving and enriching heritage languages: 'You know how to speak Spanish as a 12-year-old, as a 14-year-old, but if you don't read, you're not going to speak a rich language. You're just going to talk at a basic level. If you want your Spanish to be better, you need to read because you're out of that environment'. For families, reading bilingual books together offers a way to make language an active and engaging part of life. It fosters not only vocabulary development but also cultural understanding and the appreciation of storytelling in different languages.

Isabela, a Greek mother married to a Norwegian, illustrates how media enables her children to navigate their multilingual world. 'They talk with my mother every week in Greek, but they struggle with vocabulary, especially my youngest one', she said. 'They're not taking Greek classes because they're already learning French, Spanish and Norwegian. It's just too many languages. But Greek-language music and children's shows, along with video calls with their grandmother, keep the language alive for them'. Manuel, who grew up as a Mexican immigrant in the United States, reflects on how media played a crucial role in his own upbringing and how he now uses it with his son. 'For me, I felt that I learned English through television. In many ways, it benefited my schooling because most of my English came from either

English-speaking cousins in the US or from television, as none of my immediate family members ever spoke to me in English'. As a parent, Manuel now uses books, TV shows, and movies to help his son connect with his Mexican background and pick up some Spanish along the way.

These parents' experiences highlight how media (including books, songs music and digital tools) serves as both a resource and a strategy for raising multilingual children. Media introduces children to vocabulary, accents and cultural contexts that might otherwise be inaccessible, offering playful and engaging opportunities to learn languages. This adaptability is especially critical for families navigating uneven language fluency, as it provides a means to reinforce heritage languages while meeting the demands of daily life. For many multilingual families, media isn't just a supplement to parenting. It can really help you as you work to preserve culture and keep languages alive.

Playing with Languages

If there's one thing I've learned in raising a multilingual son, it's that language learning cannot always feel like a chore. Certainly, there are moments when it takes effort and focus, but those moments need to be balanced with joy, curiosity and fun. By making language acquisition a natural and interactive part of daily life, I've found that my family can celebrate multilingualism while building deeper cultural connections.

Translanguaging, the intentional mixing of languages introduced earlier, has also become a regular part of our lives. We don't insist on strict language separation. Rather, we treat our multilingual conversations as opportunities to explore connections between words, phrases and ideas. I might start a sentence in Czech and finish it in English or introduce a South Asian word for a concept my son finds funny or intriguing. This mirrors the approach of many multilingual families I met. When I spoke with Gabriela, she painted a vivid picture of the linguistic back and forth that unfolded in her household. She would ask her children, in Spanish, how their day had gone, only to hear their responses tumble out in English with an occasional Spanish word mixed in. This back and forth was a natural expression of their bilingual lives, not a betrayal of their heritage language. Gabriela's home became a space where Spanish and English met, mingled and adapted to the rhythms of her children's experiences. Her texts to them followed the same pattern. She crafted messages in Spanish to reinforce spelling and grammar, only to receive replies in Spanglish (a mix of Spanish and English).

In my family, we explore languages through simple games. We've added a multilingual twist to classics like Scrabble and Scattergories, adapting the rules to include words from all the languages we're learning. For instance, we allow words in any language we know and give bonus points for creative combinations or phrases. This not only keeps the game engaging but also encourages us to think across languages.

We also play language charades, where we act out phrases or words in different languages. The mix of acting and guessing inevitably leads to a lot of laughter, which helps make language learning feel light and dynamic. Another family favorite is a multilingual word chain game during dinner. We pick a category (i.e. animals) and take turns in coming up with words in as many languages as we can.

Other parents have also found creative ways to navigate multilingualism in their homes. Robin, a Mexican-American mother raising her children in the Netherlands, shared how she integrates language learning into her family's routine. 'At home, we speak mostly English, but I try to include Spanish whenever I can', Robin noted. 'It's not much, but even small things like saying goodnight in Spanish or singing nursery rhymes help keep the language alive'. To ensure her children maintain a connection to their languages, Robin enrolled them in a bilingual daycare and moved to a more international community, allowing them to naturally balance English and Dutch. By creating an environment that values multiple languages, Robin fosters her children's ability to navigate their multicultural identities.

Beyond games, my family also sometimes designates certain days for specific languages in our home. For example, 'French Fridays' or 'Czech Sundays' are dedicated to using as much of one language as possible. On those days, we greet each other in that language, play media exclusively in that language and even plan meals that tie into the culture. These themed days transform language learning into an immersive experience, encouraging discussions about culture and history while keeping things fun and low pressure.

Making It About Shared Experiences

Taking a creative approach to languages seems to be working for us right now. I've seen my son engage more deeply with his cross-cultural identity as a result. Whether it's through a silly game, a themed day or simply laughing over a word we all stumble over, language helps us feel connected to each other. The joy of multilingual parenting lies in embracing imperfection and leaning into those moments when learning feels like play.

If you are ready to commit to language learning as a priority, I commend you and refer you to many resources available to support this journey. From my own experience and conversations with other parents, I know this can feel overwhelming. Parents find it hard to balance time commitments. They may have limited financial resources. They may even feel that multilingualism is not supported where they live. So, whether you're diving in or just dipping your toes into the process, it's important to give yourself permission to approach multilingual parenting as a messy ongoing process.

Raising a multilingual child has been both a privilege and a challenge in my own life. I've realized that it's impossible to maintain all of my son's languages at the same level, and that is ok. I also realized that I needed to use all the tools I have available to me to keep the multiple languages in our home active. Media has been a great help to me. For the Czech side of things, family video calls keep the language alive, while Czech children's shows and fairy tales ground him in his heritage. Living in Los Angeles, I've also sought out opportunities for him to use Spanish, from bilingual storybooks to Spanish-language events, opening doors to new cultural spaces. Learning French alongside him through language apps and watching shows together has shown him that language learning ebbs and flows.

I am always open to new ideas and sometimes opportunities to support languages are closer than we think. Local libraries may offer multilingual story hours, and cultural meet ups create opportunities for face-to-face connections. We can pair these with digital resources like curated YouTube channels or virtual language exchanges to create an approach that works for our particular realities. We have to remember that every little bit matters. Above all, we need to celebrate progress, no matter how small. Whether it's our child finishing their first bilingual storybook, singing along to a traditional song, or laughing over a new word they've learned from a show, these moments deserve recognition.

As Gabriela shared when reflecting on her now-grown children, progress in language learning isn't always linear, but it's often more meaningful than we realize. 'It's funny. They feel more comfortable in English, but they still value their Spanish when it connects them to family. They text my mom in Spanish, they speak it when they visit her, and they've developed good spelling just by seeing the words written. Their Spanish isn't perfect, but it's enough to hold onto their roots, and that's what matters'. I could not agree more.

Notes

(1) García & Li, 2014; Williams, 2000.
(2) Gautam, 2021.
(3) Weber, 1976.
(4) Crawford, 2004.
(5) Gándara & Hopkins, 2010.
(6) Cardinal, 2004.
(7) Grin, 2003.
(8) Annamalai, 2010.
(9) De Houwer, 2009.
(10) Baker, 2007.
(11) Grosjean, 2010.
(12) García & Li, 2014; Williams, 1994.

Takeaways from Chapter 8

Languages connect across generations. Parents can share traditions and family stories using a blend of languages to help kids feel rooted in their heritage and history.

Making lessons playful can make learning stick. Whether it's a scavenger hunt for new words or a themed 'Spanish Sunday', fun activities weave language practice into everyday life.

Digital tools bring heritage languages home. Books, apps, songs and videos give children a chance to hear and use their parents' language, even when they're far from native speakers.

Mixing languages feels more real than perfection. Blending phrases and expressions from multiple tongues fills family conversations with personality and reflects the way people actually talk.

Every little step adds up to big gains. Celebrating a single new phrase or a shared story in a heritage language reminds everyone that every effort helps build lasting cultural connections.

Reflection Questions – Chapter 8

Here are five reflection questions you might consider based on the themes included in this chapter:

(1) When you think about the languages you grew up with, how have they shaped who you are and how you connect to your roots? Have there been moments when a language shift made you feel more or less at home?

(2) Do you feel it is important to pass on your heritage language or languages to your children? Why or why not?

(3) How do you balance the desire for your children to be fluent in multiple languages with everyday life?

(4) Have you had to adjust your language-related expectations along the way?

(5) How do songs, books, movies or apps in other languages help your family keep multiple languages in your home? How might a *by any media* approach help you?

Activity: Word Buffet

Purpose and Benefits

This activity promotes vocabulary building in multiple languages while fostering creativity and connections between words. It's a fun, educational and engaging game that brings the family together, making it perfect for a quick and meaningful mealtime activity.

Duration: 10–15 minutes

- Word chain gameplay: 10 minutes.
- Optional new round: 5 minutes.

What You Will Need

- A dinner table or gathering space.
- Knowledge of multiple languages (or willingness to learn new words).

How to Do It

(1) **Choose a Category:**
  - Pick a relatable category, such as animals, foods, colors or household objects.

(2) **Start the Word Chain:**
  - The first person says a word in any language related to the category (e.g. 'apple' in English).

(3) **Pass the Turn:**
  - The next person says a related word but in a different language.
  - The word doesn't need to be a direct translation. It can be a concept or object connected to the previous word.

(4) **Keep Going:**
  - Continue the chain, ensuring each word is connected to the last, and each person speaks in a different language.
  - Offer help with translations if needed to keep the game moving.

(5) **Challenge Rule (Optional):**
  - Add a rule that no one can use the same language twice in a round to push participants to think creatively across multiple languages.

(6) **Set a Time Limit:**
  - Each round should take a few minutes. If players exhaust all possibilities, choose a new category for fresh connections.

Example Round (Category: Food)

- **Player 1 (English):** 'Apple'.
- **Player 2 (Spanish):** 'Fruta' (Fruit).
- **Player 3 (French):** 'Rouge' (Red, describing the apple).

- **Player 4 (German)**: 'Saft' (Juice, connected to apples).
- **Player 5 (Italian)**: 'Dolce' (Sweet, describing the taste of apples).

Reflection or Follow-Up (Optional)

- What new words or languages did you learn during the game?
- How can this activity encourage language learning or cross-cultural understanding in everyday life?
- Would you like to explore new categories or add more challenge rules in the next round?

Part 4
Build and Sustain
Connection Across Distance

9 Seek Out Communities

Figure 9.1 Don't be afraid to blend media when it comes to finding cross-cultural communities. (credit A. Desai)

It was a crisp Saturday morning in December. We had gotten up early to drive to the Czech School in Los Angeles so Marek could take part in their annual Mikuláš (Saint Nicholas) holiday celebration. We stood in line and then it was time for my son to go in to see Mikuláš and Čert (Saint Nicholas and the Devil, brought to life by parent volunteers). They were in full costume and addressed him by name, asking him if he had been nice to his parents all year. Marek answered their questions and walked away with a big smile and bag of candy. As I followed him out of the room, I exchanged knowing looks with other parents. Making this event happen had been a joint effort and every member of our local Czech community had pitched in. We all wanted our children to connect to their heritage, which is why we had sought out the Czech School of Los Angeles, an informal and largely volunteer-run organization.

For several years (before COVID-19 hit) the school and community became central to my family's cross-cultural lives.

The Czech School offered more than just weekly language classes. It was also a social space that helped us connect with Czech culture when Marek was small. From egg painting on Easter to organized camping trips, the school created a space where our cross-cultural identities could flourish. My son crafted, learned folk songs and even dressed in costume for cultural events. Not every family was strictly Czech. There were many mixed couples in the community, which made the sense of connection over our shared diasporic experience even more helpful.

From formal organizations to more informal spaces, cross-cultural communities can take many forms. The Indian side of our cross-cultural lives is actually mostly tied to my husband's extended family who we see on major holidays and family events. Though it feels lighter touch for sure, it is still extremely important for Marek to have these connections and to understand them. He has asked my husband many questions about his family and learned a lot from his uncles and cousins.

That said, cross-cultural community isn't just something I found in person. A few months into being a parent, I realized that I needed more advice, resources and perspectives, especially when it came to raising a multilingual child. So, like all good parents, I turned to online communities and social media for help (I say this with a small touch of irony, but not much). I sought out advice and support from multilingual parent groups on social media. These virtual spaces, often populated by parents from around the world, offered an unexpectedly valuable form of emotional support. In these online spaces, I found parents who were just like me. They were grappling with how to balance multiple languages. They wondered if their children were learning quickly enough. They debated the best strategies for fostering fluency in more than one language. The connections I have made online, though less formal and distant, have been equally vital in shaping my cross-cultural parenting journey. I really could not have done it alone.

So, this chapter is a little different from the other ones in this book. Here, I focus on how parents augment their cross-cultural parenting by finding supportive communities. For many of the parents I met, myself included, these communities provide a crucial sense of connection, solidarity and shared understanding. All of these supports are crucial if we are to maintain and sustain our cross-cultural commitments.

Everyday conversations in these real and virtual spaces often serve as invaluable learning moments. Parents discuss how to approach language learning, hold onto traditions or cultural traditions, or even how to navigate cultural conflict in the home. Yet, seeking out these communities doesn't always happen naturally. In today's world, where the demands of work and parenting often leave little room for casual social interactions, it can be easy to feel isolated. I have definitely felt this way. On top of it, cross-cultural parents often live far away from family. This makes them feel the need for community even more urgent. Whether these communities exist in a physical space, like the Czech School of Los Angeles, or in virtual spaces on social media, they can really be very important. I would even go so far as to say that they can become lifelines where parents can share knowledge, seek advice and, most importantly, remind each other that they are not alone.

In-Person Communities: Finding Local Support Networks

Many parents I met mentioned in-person communities that support them when it comes to cross-cultural parenting. Like me, some parents sought out these communities once they became parents. I admit I had no idea that there were so many Czechs in Los Angeles until I became a mother! Others were part of these communities even before they became parents. Rachel, an Israeli who raised her children in the US for several years, also sought out a supportive community to sustain Israeli culture in her family. For her, it was the weekly Israeli community gatherings in Los Angeles, the shared dinners and holiday celebrations.

For Rachel, this community was part of a larger by any media repertoire of activities. Language was a priority, so she insisted on speaking Hebrew with her children. She also made it a point to provide Hebrew books for her children to read. For Rachel, cross-cultural parenting was also tied to Jewish rituals like doing blessings for Shabbat. But, it was also about small acts like shopping for challah (bread) together.

Rachel realized just how important all of these small actions were when her children began interacting with other cross-cultural Israeli kids in the local park. They were able to communicate in Hebrew (with some English mixed in) and realized that their family was not the only one living like this. Seeing these interactions and connecting with other parents helped Rachel find Israeli cultural touchpoints in her family's everyday life.

Rachel's community became about much more than cultural heritage and provided emotional support for her and her family, especially when she and her husband were trying to decide whether they should return to Israel. She was able to talk through her reasoning with other families who understood what was at stake. She realized that she wasn't the only one grappling with these questions and facing decisions that would greatly impact her family. Ultimately, Rachel and her family did decide to return to their homeland. Looking back at that moment years later, Rachel believes that the community in Los Angeles really helped prepare her and her children for this move.

This sense of connection and shared support highlights the significance of what sociologist Ray Oldenburg calls 'third places', social spaces like parks, places of worship, cafes, restaurants and theaters that are outside our homes (first places) and places of work (second places).[1] I have learned that third places can be extremely important for cross-cultural parents. They can become places where children can encounter their cultural heritage and cultural traditions. They can also become places where parents and children connect with each other around cultural activities. And, perhaps most importantly they provide opportunities for cross-cultural parents to connect with other parents who understand their priorities and experiences. At their best, cross-cultural third spaces can be flexible and welcoming. Parents can opt in when they can and participate in ways that make sense to them. They can meet people they would have otherwise not met.

I can attest firsthand that cross-cultural third places are very conducive to connecting with communities as interactions weren't formal or structured. Conversations happen over shared meals. People learn about each other gradually. For many parents, it was actually the informal nature of these third space cross-cultural communities that made them so powerful. They were able to build trust and social connection in serendipitous ways that are not easy to replicate in more formally organized spaces. They noted that this was because people were relaxed, they let down their guard. They wanted to reach out and share their experiences with others who understood their situation. Ultimately, they want to know they belong.

While the initial goal of such commuinity-centered places may often be cultural preservation, the parents I met often saw them as much more. They mentioned that they made friends, which is something that can be very hard to do at any age and especially if you are a cross-cultural family. They were also able to get advice and emotional support. These are not formal support groups. These are informal networks of cross-cultural families who, over time, share experiences, build trust and support each other.

For me, the impromptu conversations during camping trips, Mommy Christmas baking sessions and casual meetings in a park helped me connect with other cross-cultural parents. Through these encounters I learned about multilingual parenting strategies, places that sold ingredients I needed to make a culturally specific dish, and other families celebrated holidays in their own blended cultural contexts. In these everyday cross-cultural community interactions, I found the support I needed, often when I least expected it.

Building Your Own Community: Using Cross-Cultural Experiences to Connect

While communities like the Czech School of Los Angeles can be sources of support, not every parent has access to an existing cultural network in their local area. In fact, many cross-cultural parents live in places where there are few or no people who share their cultural background. This was the case for Gabriela, who moved from Chile to Bowling Green, Kentucky, when her husband got a job there. Bowling Green does not have a large Chilean community. Given this reality, Gabriela had to think more creatively and look for connections within the broader Latin-American community.

'I met people from Mexico, Peru, Argentina, and we got together because we spoke the same language', Gabriela recalls. While the group wasn't specifically Chilean, speaking Spanish and a shared Latin-American heritage helped her form the community she needed. Like Rachel, Gabriela's Latin-American community in Bowling green also organized regular gatherings to help parents and children connect to their cultural roots, more regionally defined.

Jana had a similar experience when she first moved to Los Angeles from the Czech Republic years ago. When she arrived, she didn't initially find other Czech families. Instead, her sense of belonging came from the international community she discovered through the French International School of Los Angeles that her children attended. 'I became very involved with the school', Jana explains, 'and through those connections, I found families from all over the world who shared the experience of being far from home'. In sharing this experience, Jana hits on something very important. Whether it was a parent from France, Brazil or Japan, the common thread of navigating life in a new country, raising children in a foreign cultural context and maintaining ties to one's heritage created a bond that transcends cultural and national backgrounds. This shared experience of crossing cultures, even if those cultures are different, can be incredibly helpful in finding a supportive community for those of us parenting across cultures.

When the parents I met couldn't find the exact match for their cultural background, they sometimes took a broader multicultural or multilingual approach. Thinking creatively about community building can be the key to overcoming isolation. You don't just have to seek out others who share your exact cultural background, you can widen your search to include other multicultural families who share similar experiences of navigating cross-cultural identities. Often, these spaces can offer just as much, if not more, support.

When no established local community exists, you may even consider forming your own. This can feel daunting, but it is often one of the most empowering decisions a parent can make. This was Aaila's experience. As an Afghan immigrant in Kentucky, she realized that her community was small and isolated. She was daunted at first but then decided to take action. 'We bring all the women together twice a week', Aaila explains, 'and they are happy to share their experiences'. Working with a local organization, Aaila now runs meetings for recently arrived Afghan women to offer emotional and practical support. She also leads these meetings to help the women connect with each other and feel less alone as they navigate life in a new country.

Virtual Communities: The Role of Online Support Networks

Some cross-cultural parents turn to online platforms like Facebook, TikTok, X and WhatsApp to find community. Hannah, an American missionary mother raising her children in Djibouti, reflects on how blogging and online connections transformed her parenting journey. 'Around 2011 or 2012, blogging really took off', she recalls. 'I wrote a post about parenting Third Culture Kids, and it reached a lot of people in my little world. Other parents began reaching out to me, including authors like Ruth Van Reken. Suddenly, I had access to this vast wealth of resources and a community of parents experiencing similar challenges'. For Hannah, the internet and social media enabled her to share her cross-cultural experiences and learn from other parents. Countless forums, apps, and dedicated websites now offer support to cross-cultural parents. There are groups dedicated to bilingualism, to cultural heritage, and even to navigating time zones. Websites like the platform launched by Alyssa, a self-identified Third Culture Kid originally from Cameroon, specifically target communities that often feel underrepresented in traditional expat spaces. These platforms not only offer advice and resources but also create spaces where parents can share their stories and feel seen. I have turned to virtual communities many times. Parenting forums and multilingual groups on Facebook have all become essential spaces where I can share concerns, ask questions and exchange experiences with other parents who are navigating similar realties. Just a click away (so to speak), convenience is key here.

And, it's not all about the children. I have turned to these communities to find support for my own cross-cultural journey. I once made a particularly meaningful connection through a psychologist-led Facebook group that focuses on how challenging it can be to move abroad. In this group, we explore the dangers of diasporic nostalgia, idealizing the past and failing to fully engage with the present. Conversations also delved into the evolving and complicated meaning of 'home' for those who move often. That one hit me hard as I always say that home is where someone is waiting for me.

Such virtual communities tend to foster 'weak ties', or occasional and casual interactions.[2] Though the parents I met often dismissed such ties as peripheral or largely symbolic, they have the potential to be quite influential and significant. As I already discussed, in-person communities are often based on shared spaces ('third places') and personal relationships. Virtual communities are not place-based and can easily facilitate a vast array of interests and commitments. You might interact with people once or many times. They may offer you advice or answer questions you have. They may offer you words of support when you describe a problem you are facing. You may consider what they say and dismiss it outright, or you may find their support and advice helpful.

Alyssa found solace and solidarity through online chats with other TCKs via X (formerly Twitter). She joined the TCK community chat, where people across generations, from teenagers to those in their 60s, came together to share their cross-cultural experiences. Alyssa explains. 'There were people from ages 19 to 65 all bonding over similar experiences'. These conversations didn't need the intimacy of face-to-face interactions as they were about making the shared experiences of being a TCK visible. People posted about navigating multiple cultural identities. They posted how hard it can be to move between countries. They shared strategies for maintaining relationships across borders. Over time, these shared stories and expressions of support by those who read them led to a mutual understanding among those participating. In this X thread, 'weak ties' led to lasting connections between people who understood the unique circumstances that those who participated faced.

Of course, virtual communities come with both pros and cons. While these networks provide an essential form of emotional support, they can lack the depth of real-world communities. As sociologist Sherry Turkle notes, what we gain in convenience and accessibility, we lose when it comes to continuity and deeper meaning.[3] Virtual communities may answer questions quickly. They may put our minds at ease in the moment. But without consistent and meaningful engagement, we may still need to seek out the emotional bonds that in-person communities can foster. For cross-cultural parents, this can be both an advantage and a disadvantage. On the one hand, parents may find that tapping into a vast virtual community offers a unique form of flexibility. If you have a pressing question about bilingual language development or want to vent about the difficulties of maintaining cultural traditions, online communities can provide an immediate response. On the other hand, these interactions can sometimes feel fleeting and are vulnerable to misunderstandings. Without the ability to see people face to face or engage in long-term relationships, the emotional depth of these connections may be limited.

Still, the pros of virtual communities far outweigh the cons for many parents. If real-world communities are hard to find, online platforms provide a valuable alternative. A parent in a rural area, for example, can connect with families in major cities or even other countries to gain new insights into cross-cultural parenting strategies. Virtual communities are also more accommodating when it comes to scheduling. Parents can log on during their lunch break or after the kids are in bed. Virtual communities may provide diverse experiences and perspectives that might not be available locally. While virtual communities may not always provide the same level of emotional depth as real-world connections, they are still essential to many parents.

Benedict Anderson's (1983) *Imagined Communities* provide us with another way to think about finding our virtual cross-cultural communities. Much like Anderson's idea that a nation is a socially constructed community, imagined through common values, cross-cultural parent communities enable parents to share what they have in common. In these spaces, parents may never meet face to face, yet they form strong bonds rooted in an imagined community, shared goals and collective learning.

I have discovered first-hand how transformative these communities can be. As someone navigating my Czech and Nepali heritage, while also embracing the Indian-American identity that I now share with my son, these spaces are more than theoretical constructs. They are lifelines. They are where I turn for advice on teaching Marek Czech grammar, for discussions about how to balance his exposure to Indian cultural practices and even for recipes that allow us to bridge these worlds on our dinner table. Whether it's troubleshooting Marek's struggles with language retention, finding strategies to celebrate cultural festivals in ways that feel authentic or simply sharing the challenges of raising a child across multiple cultures, these communities have become vital.

For many parents, imagining this sense of community is the first step in building one, whether envisioning a local group of multicultural families or finding an online network that reflects their unique experiences. Even before the first message is sent or the first meetup occurs, the act of imagining a supportive community lays the foundation for meaningful connection.

Combining Real and Virtual: Blending Communities

Ultimately, most parents want to strike a balance between real-world and virtual communities and the best of both worlds. So, they blend the immediacy and accessibility of online platforms with the deeper, more personal bonds formed through in-person gatherings.

Take the case of Ingrid, who grew up between cultures and is now raising her cross-cultural son. In other words, she has given cross-cultural parenting a lot of thought. She shared that blended communities have been crucial to her parenting journey. Locally, Ingrid meets up with friends who also grew up internationally or are in cross-cultural relationships. She then turns to virtual communities to stay connected with her family friends and see what other cross-cultural parents are doing. 'Facebook has been an amazing resource', Ingrid explained,

'It's one of the only reasons I get on Facebook. I want to check out where people are internationally that I don't have any other way of keeping in touch with'. In fact, platforms like WhatsApp, Zoom and Facebook have helped her to maintain bonds and form new ones. For Ingrid, sharing cultural heritage with her son has also been a key part of this balance. She used digital photo slideshows to tell her son stories about her childhood in Nepal. Over time, these screenings became a family tradition. 'He loves those stories', Ingrid says, noting that he now shares them with his friends with pride. These virtual connections and digital screenings complement Ingrid's in-person support network.

Whether online or in-person, cross-cultural parents like Ingrid constantly learn from each other and from the broader communities. In virtual communities, parents might share resources for teaching children a second language, exchange stories about cultural traditions or discuss strategies for keeping cultural ties strong. These online interactions offer a platform for continuous learning and connection, even when physical proximity is not possible.

In-person communities allow for direct, embodied experiences of cultural traditions and practices. For Ingrid's son, the diversity he encounters through local networks helps him understand of what it means to belong to a multicultural family. By tapping both virtual and in-person communities, Ingrid has created what Etienne Wenger would call a well-rounded 'community of practice' for herself. This means she has set up an array of connections that help her share knowledge, engage in common practices and build collective meaning.[4] Like Ingrid, other parents also create their own uniquely blended communities, that exist in virtual spaces as much as they do in in-person ones.

Practical Benefits of Community: Advice, Resources and Support

So, to sum things up, speaking with parents taught me that both real and virtual communities offer immense practical benefits for us as cross-cultural parents. This is where we can seek out advice. This is where we can share resources. This is where we offer each other emotional support. This is where we as parents can offer each other emotional support as we navigate the unique challenges of raising children in a multicultural environment, including teaching heritage languages to balancing cultural traditions with pressures to integrate. While each parent's experience within these networks may be different, the core elements that make these communities rewarding are largely the same.

In both real and virtual communities, the connections we make can help us feel that we belong. Our everyday interactions in these spaces, whether online or in-person, provide us with practical help and emotional comfort. Many of the parents I met, for example, rely on friends and family networks for ongoing support. These networks don't exist in formal settings; instead, they emerge from casual gatherings, conversations at family events or playdates with children. Benjamin's cross-cultural family, with ties to both Nepali and Austrian traditions, regularly turns to friends in their community for advice. He asks about new restaurants, about blending different holiday traditions and about finding local resources for cultural activities. These brief encounters can provide valuable insights. A conversation at a cultural festival or a meetup at a park might give people ideas. A lot of learning and support takes place within these casual encounters.

That said, finding communities can be hard. Cross-cultural parents often face obstacles in connecting with other similar families. They may have time constraints. They approach the nuances of cross-cultural parenting differently from others in the group. They may have financial limitations. They may not have the language skills needed to become part of a group. They may even face prejudice and discrimination. Finding or creating a community that reflects one's cultural background, values and parenting goals can be time consuming, especially for parents who are already balancing the demands of work, family and life in a new country. Cultural differences can also pose a challenge, as parents might struggle to find common ground with others in their community who come from different backgrounds or hold different beliefs about parenting.

Tammi, a parent with Dominican and American roots, faced many of these challenges while trying to create a cross-cultural support network for herself. Her experience involved balancing multiple cultural influences, not just from her own background but from the diverse friends and communities she sought out. For Tammi, building a community meant reaching out to other multicultural families, even if they didn't share her exact heritage. She found it hard at first as people tended to group themselves based on their cultural heritage, not based on their lived cross-cultural experiences. She persisted and over time, she found her people virtually and in-person. Although her path to building this network was not straightforward, Tammi found that the rewards of community far outweighed the challenges.

Distance and cultural complexity can make cross-cultural parenting feel like a daunting task. This is why virtual AND in-person communities are so important for cross-cultural parents. They are spaces of emotional and practical support. This is where we can share our stories and know they will be understood. This is where we are reminded that we are not navigating this journey alone. A network of solidarity, connection and mutual care may just be a click, or a park gathering, away.

Notes

(1) Oldenburg, 1999.
(2) Granovetter, 1973.
(3) Turkle, 2012.
(4) Wenger, 1998.

Takeaways from Chapter 9

Local communities can bring support. Parents can seek out formal and informal cultural communities to meet like-minded people, participate in events and give their children in-person cross-cultural experiences.

Online networks step in when needed. When local resources are scarce, parents find advice, encouragement and fresh ideas in digital spaces and virtual communities.

Facing challenges together strengthens bonds. Connecting with other cross-cultural families, even those from different backgrounds, can offer solidarity, practical tips and the reassurance that you're not alone.

Building community starts with one idea. If no local communities exist, parents can bring people together. Whether it's a potluck, playgroup or shared-interest meetup, small events can become a trusted cultural space.

Combining real and virtual keeps support within reach. Blending face-to-face meetups with online groups gives families both hands-on activities and emotional backing, no matter where they live.

Reflection Questions – Chapter 9

Here are five reflection questions you might consider based on the themes included in this chapter:

(1) What communities do you currently connect with? In-person? Virtually?

(2) What role do in-person and virtual communities currently play in your cross-cultural life and parenting?

(3) Do your in-person communities and online groups complement each other? Have digital platforms opened doors to cultural traditions or conversations you couldn't easily find where you live?

(4) Which cultural traditions or values feel most important for your child to carry forward? Have you found that in-person or virtual community spaces can help?

(5) Are you struggling in any way when it comes to your cross-cultural parenting and family? Could finding a community that shares your background or interests help?

Activity: Charting Your Connections

Purpose and Benefits

This activity helps families map their existing support networks and identify gaps to better understand and strengthen their connections. By visualizing current communities and imagining new ones, participants can take actionable steps to create a stronger, more supportive network for cross-cultural parenting.

Duration: 30–45 minutes

- Mapping and reflecting: 20–25 minutes.
- Planning and action steps: 10–15 minutes.

What You Will Need

- A piece of paper for each participant.
- Colored markers or pens.

How to Do It

(1) **Create a Community Map:**
- Draw a circle in the center of your paper to represent you and your family.
- From this center, draw lines radiating out to other circles representing the communities you currently have access to.
- Label these circles with names of communities or specific people/groups, such as:
  o Local, in-person communities (e.g. school parent groups, cultural associations, religious groups).
  o Virtual communities (e.g. online forums, Facebook groups, WhatsApp communities).
  o Friends and family (e.g. extended family members, close friends with shared cultural experiences).

(2) **Identify Types of Support:**
- Reflect on what type of support each community provides, and label the circles with these categories, such as:
  o Emotional comfort.
  o Practical parenting advice.
  o Language learning.
  o Cultural connection.
  o Bilingual education resources.

(3) **Reflect on Gaps:**
- Examine your map and ask:
  o Are there areas where you feel unsupported?
  o Are there communities you wish you had access to, such as a heritage language group or a multicultural parenting group?
- Mark these gaps on your map for further reflection.

(4) Imagine New Communities:
- Think of potential communities that could fill the gaps you identified.
- Add new circles to your map, labeled with these imagined communities (e.g. local cultural events, virtual interest groups).
- Use Benedict Anderson's concept of 'Imagined Communities' to envision networks you could create or join.

(5) Take Action:
- Identify one real-world or virtual community you'd like to engage with more fully.
- Research ways to connect with this group, such as attending a meeting, joining an online forum or reaching out to someone in your network.
- Write down a specific action step to take within the next week.

Reflection or Follow-Up (Optional)

- Did you discover more community support than you initially realized?
- What are the most important types of support you need as a cross-cultural parent?
- How can you strengthen your connection to existing communities or begin building new ones?

10 Visit and Connect, Even Virtually

Figure 10.1 Don't be afraid to get creative when it comes to connecting with family across distance. (credit A. Desai)

It's early morning and my 10-year-old son, Marek, is already on his iPad. The screen glows softly as he waits for the familiar FaceTime ring. Soon, my mother and father in the Czech Republic answer. They exchange greetings, then dive into their routine: browsing the week's supermarket deals. Marek shares his screen, pulling up the latest Kaufland flyer on Kaufland.cz. Together, they carefully scan the items, comparing discounts and making notes. Once their list is finalized, Marek sends it over in an iMessage, so my parents are fully prepared for their next shopping trip.

This ritual has evolved from a simple habit they started during our last summer visit to the Czech Republic. Back then, Marek would help my parents sift through the paper flyers delivered to their mailbox, circling the best deals. Now, even though he's back in Los Angeles and too far to continue this in-person, they've brought the tradition online. The screen between them seems to melt away as they laugh about their shared finds. Later, they'll call back and review how their shopping adventure went, comparing prices, successes and misses.

As I watch Marek effortlessly connect with his grandparents, I once again note how casual and seamless it feels. Video calls, instant messaging, screen sharing, all of these tools allow us to collapse the distance, bringing the ordinary details of life into real-time conversations. Families like mine can continue to participate in each other's lives in ways that were unimaginable just a generation ago.

However, as transformative as these tools are, they also present limitations. Just as I was drafting this chapter, Marek came to me with a question that broke my heart. 'Is there any way we can go and visit babička and děda [grandma and grandpa] in the next few weeks?' he asked, his tone a mix of longing and resignation. 'FaceTime is not the same', he sighed when I shook my head. Like him I know too well that feeling of distance when the call ends that lingers long after the screen goes dark. I too dread the abrupt return to reality where loved ones are still across oceans.

Still, I am acutely aware of the privilege we have in being able to travel to visit them regularly, even if it is not as often as we would like. The opportunity to bridge that distance, however fleeting, is something I do not take for granted. Many of the parents I met on this journey have no such option. For some, financial constraints, political barriers or immigration restrictions make visiting loved ones impossible. For others, even the hope of seeing family again feels out of reach. Virtual interactions are all they have.

This reality was particularly acute for the Afghan refugees I met in Kentucky. Fleeing their homeland in the wake of conflict and political upheaval, these families faced not only the trauma of displacement but also the heartbreak of separation. For many, their loved ones remain in Afghanistan or scattered across countries like Germany, Australia or Canada. They can only be reached through intermittent video calls or text messages. For the Afghan refugees and others in similar situations, the limitations of technology are magnified. Virtual tools may offer moments of connection, but they cannot ease the ache of long-term separation or fill the void left by a fractured sense of belonging. Their resilience in maintaining ties despite these challenges is deeply inspiring. It also reminds us of the vast disparities in what cross-cultural families can access when it comes to staying connected.

So, I need to be honest: relying on virtual tools to maintain relationships is a bittersweet reality. These technologies act as both a bridge and a reminder of what's missing. They allow us to stay connected across distances impossible to envision in the previous generation, but they also emphasize the absence of shared physical spaces, the smell of home-cooked meals and the spontaneous moments that lie at the heart of our deepest bonds. For families like mine, the challenge lies in navigating this duality. I choose to embrace the possibilities that technology provides while holding space for the ache it cannot soothe.

In this chapter, I explore how cross-cultural families use technology to bridge distance to keep in touch with relatives and friends in other geographies. From video calls that bring loved ones into our daily lives to virtual tours that preserve cultural traditions, media technologies offer remarkable ways to stay connected. Yet, as many parents shared with me, these virtual experiences are just one part of the equation. The emotional weight of physical separation persists. This is a reality that families must grapple with as they work to maintain relationships and cultural heritage across borders. Marisol, a mother from Costa Rica, reflected on how much easier it would have been to stay connected when her children were young if tools like WhatsApp had existed. 'I wish WhatsApp was already developed when my mom and dad were alive', she sighed. 'They would have enjoyed my kids so much more. It would be so much easier to communicate'.

Daily Communication: The Power of Video Calls

For the vast majority of the parents I met, video calls have become an indispensable cost-effective tool, allowing them to stay connected despite being separated by oceans and time zones. Whether they are daily, weekly or even monthly, these virtual check-ins provide comfort and routine, bridging not only the physical distance but also the emotional gap that can widen when family members are far from home. Tammi, originally from the Dominican Republic and now living in Vermont, reflects on how Skype once played a crucial role in keeping her family connected across continents. 'Back then, it was all about Skype', she recalls, 'We'd gather around the computer, much like this, and it was the only way to connect to family and friends in distant places'.

More recently, Gabriela, who moved from Chile to the United States for her husband's job, found that maintaining close ties with her family back home was essential to preserving her children's connection to their Chilean roots. Early on, she discovered the power of WhatsApp to keep those relationships alive. 'With WhatsApp, I can send pictures immediately... it's much faster', she explains. It's not just about staying in touch. It's about maintaining a real-time window into each other's lives. Her children can share milestones with their Chilean relatives, whether it's sending a snapshot of a school project or sharing a quick video from a family outing. This ability to share everyday mundane and significant moments creates a feeling of presence that transcends the distance.

Aaila, an Afghan immigrant living in Bowling Green, Kentucky, also relies on video calls to maintain her family's cultural connection with family spread across the globe. 'We keep in touch with family in Germany, Australia and Denmark through WhatsApp and Skype', she says. These regular calls give her and her daughters a chance to practice their language skills, hear family stories and stay engaged with Afghan traditions.

Living in an area with few other Afghan families, Aaila is acutely aware of how easily those cultural connections could fade. Her daughters are now growing up in a largely American context, and without the regular influence of extended family, it would be easy for them to lose touch with their Afghan heritage. Through these calls, her daughters get to hear about everyday life in Afghanistan and other parts of the world where their relatives live. The video calls also allow her daughters to maintain relationships with relatives and immerse themselves in the language and culture that Aaila holds dear.

These daily interactions create a steady rhythm for Gabriela and Aaila's families, one that offers reassurance and connection amidst the uncertainty of living far from home. Research on intergenerational communication in general supports these experiences, as video calls enable families to maintain a level of closeness and immediacy that would otherwise be difficult to achieve across such great distances.[1]

Technology as a Bridge Across Generations

For cross-cultural families, maintaining bonds between children and their grandparents can be one of the most rewarding yet challenging aspects of family life. Grandparents, and other older family members, often play a vital role in passing down traditions, values and family stories – connections that are critical to a child's sense of identity. However, physical separation, whether across countries or continents, can strain these relationships.

This phenomenon is by no means exclusive to cross-cultural families. Even when families live within the same country, grandparents and grandchildren are often not co-located. For example, Marek also regularly uses FaceTime to speak with Nani (his other grandmother), who lives just an hour away by plane in northern California. Overhearing their calls, they often revolve around what they ate, saw and worked on that day. They are beautiful in that they are so casual, almost like Marek just popped in next door to say, 'Hello'. While Marek and Nani do see each other in-person more frequently than many cross-cultural families, the ability to maintain a consistent connection between visits has still helped them keep up with each other's daily lives.

Jessica is raising her children with Irish and Argentinian heritage in the United States. She has also found WhatsApp to be a vital tool for fostering her daughter's connection with her grandmother in Argentina. 'One of my twins rings her grandmother in Argentina regularly on WhatsApp', Jessica shared. These calls are more than conversations. They are opportunities to share family history, hear stories of life in Argentina and keep cultural traditions alive. For Jessica's daughter, the regular calls help her maintain a sense of closeness that might otherwise fade.

What is particularly remarkable here is just how much older generations have embraced tools like WhatsApp and FaceTime to stay connected. Research by Sonia Livingstone, Alicia Blum-Ross and others highlights how many grandparents have adapted to these technologies despite initial challenges, driven by their deep desire to stay involved in their grandchildren's lives.[2] For cross-cultural families, this technological bridge holds particular significance, as it enables children to maintain ties to their heritage while fostering relationships across generations. Yet, as Marek's experience with Nani demonstrates, this is a development with universal implications.

Creative Virtual Interactions: More Than Just Talking

Some parents also encourage their children and relatives to get creative with their video chats, going well beyond simple conversation. This is the case for Mai, who is originally from Vietnam and now lives in the Netherlands. She has taken video calls between her daughter and her relatives in Vietnam to the next level. Rather than simply chatting, her daughter asks her aunt to draw stories during their video calls. As the camera focuses on her aunt's hands, sketching out scenes and characters, Mai's daughter follows along, laughing and asking questions. This interactive storytelling brings them closer, allowing Mai's daughter to immerse herself in Vietnamese culture in a way that feels both engaging and personal. The drawings become a bridge between two worlds, connecting Mai's daughter to her heritage in real time, even though they are thousands of miles apart.

Similarly, Lyla, originally from Serbia, has found a creative way to share her homeland with her children, even though they have yet to visit in-person. Unable to travel back for a variety of reasons, Lyla uses YouTube videos to give her children a virtual tour of Serbia. They sit together, watching travel vlogs of people exploring the streets of towns Lyla knows well, wandering through markets, mountains and coastal areas. It's not the same as being there, but it allows her children to experience the sights and sounds of their mother's country. Through these virtual tours, Lyla's children have developed a familiarity with the places she talks about, and they can visualize what life might be like there, even though they've never set foot in that country.

This concept of 'virtual tourism' is not unique to cross-cultural families. Over the past few years, virtual travel experiences have become increasingly popular, allowing people to explore far-off places without leaving their homes. According to Daniel Guttentag, virtual tourism provides a means of simulating real-world travel experiences through digital media, offering a valuable tool for those unable to physically visit certain locations.[3] During the COVID-19 pandemic, this concept gained even more traction as people around the world turned to virtual tours to stay connected to global cultures and destinations they couldn't reach. For families like Lyla's, this approach serves an additional purpose: it allows children to explore their cultural heritage when in-person visits aren't feasible.

The Emotional Realities of Distance

As video calls and other digital tools become central to the cross-cultural parenting experience, they often bring with them an emotional weight that's difficult to ignore. Parents and children alike feel the gap between virtual presence and the intimacy of being physically together. No matter how seamless the technology or frequent calls, the emotional realities of distance can't always be bridged by a screen.

Ramona knows this feeling all too well. As a Taiwanese-American woman raising her family in the United States, maintaining her connection to Taiwan has been a deeply personal challenge. Growing up, she spent summers in Taiwan with her grandparents, creating a strong bond and rich cultural memories. But now, as a parent herself, she recognizes how different it feels to rely on virtual communication to maintain these ties.

'We used to make monthly phone calls to Taiwan when I was a child', Ramona recalls. 'Those calls were precious, but nothing compared to the summers we spent together in-person'. Recently, she took her children on a trip to Taiwan, where they met extended family for the first time. For Ramona, this trip was a chance for her children to immerse themselves in the culture and to see a side of her they had never known. As valuable as virtual tools are for keeping the connection alive, Ramona knows they can't replace the experience of being physically present. Her children may enjoy learning about their heritage through apps or hearing about Taiwan from her stories, but the trip brought them face-to-face with relatives and gave them an opportunity to experience local realities.

This is why Layla, whom I introduced in Chapter 3, makes it a point to visit Egypt with her children once a year, spending at least a month reconnecting with family. The yearly trips are a cornerstone of their cultural identity, giving her children a chance to fully immerse themselves in their Egyptian roots. But in the months between these visits, Layla also relies heavily on video calls to maintain the connection with her parents and extended family. 'We make sure they talk to their grandparents every week via video call', she says, acknowledging the importance of maintaining these relationships, even if only virtually.

While these video calls provide a sense of continuity, Layla admits they aren't enough. The joy of visiting Egypt is irreplaceable. There is the smell of familiar foods. The bustle and warmth of family gatherings. The intense traffic experiences. Her children love hearing their grandparents' voices, but they also long for the time they spend together in-person. For Layla, there's a constant tension between gratitude for the technology that keeps them connected and a deep sense of loss for the moments that can only be shared in person. The distance weighs heavily on her, and she knows her children feel it too.

This emotional complexity is something many cross-cultural parents grapple with. On the one hand, technology offers an incredible opportunity to maintain family bonds that would otherwise fade with time and distance. On the other hand, it highlights the limitations of virtual interactions. Mirca Madianou, Sondra Cuban and others highlight this paradox of digital communication in transnational families: while technology enables vital connections across distances, it also amplifies the sense of separation.[4] Seeing and hearing loved ones through a screen can bring comfort but simultaneously emphasize the lack of physical closeness, which no digital tool can fully replicate.

For families like Ramona's and Layla's, the emotional realities of distance often surface during the quiet moments after a video call ends. Like me, other parents see the flicker of disengagement on their children's faces when the screen goes dark. No amount of virtual interaction can replace the act of hugging a grandparent, or the shared laughter over a meal in the same room. These are the moments that shape childhood memories and deepen family bonds in ways that technology, no matter how advanced, simply cannot.

It's important for parents to acknowledge these feelings, both for themselves and for their children. The longing for in-person connection is natural, and trying to suppress or ignore it only amplifies the emotional weight of distance. Managing these emotions requires a delicate balance. It's about making the most of the technology available while recognizing its limits. Parents can help their children cope by creating rituals around virtual interactions that enhance the sense of connection, whether that's making a weekly video call a special event or planning a future visit to look forward to. In doing so, families can navigate the emotional landscape of distance with more resilience, knowing that while technology can't replace in-person interactions, it can still play a crucial role in maintaining the ties that matter most.

Blending Virtual and In-Person Cultural Exposure

Blending travel and virtual visits to maintain cultural connections is rarely seamless. For families navigating cross-cultural lives, the realization that neither they nor the places they visit are unchanged can be jarring. As the Czech saying goes, *'Do stejné řeky dvakrát nevstoupíš'* (you cannot step into the same river twice). The country you visit is not the one you left, and you and your children are not the same as when you departed. These shifts require families to approach both virtual and in-person connections with intention, recognizing that what they are creating is not a return to a static 'home' but a relationship with an evolving place, culture and self.

Diaspora studies have focused on the concept of imagined homelands and the role nostalgia plays in shaping our perceptions of cultural identity. If I were to summarize their findings in a few words, I would say that there is strong evidence that the diasporic experience changes our relationship with our former homelands and distorts our memories of it as well. For parents, this can pose challenges in fostering their children's relationship to their cross-cultural selves. The homeland that parents carry in their memories may no longer exist, and the tension between those memories and the lived realities of returning can be profound. Virtual visits and regular communication can help families navigate these challenges, offering a way to stay connected to evolving cultural landscapes while preparing for the complexities of in-person interactions.

Benjamin's family also reflects on this interplay between virtual and real-world connections. During the Nepali civil war, virtual tools became indispensable for staying in touch with relatives and maintaining cultural ties. However, returning to Nepal after the war underscored how much had changed for the country, their family and their children. 'We visited Nepal during the civil war, and it was quite frightening with army presence everywhere', Benjamin recalls. These visits, layered with the virtual connections they had maintained, reinforced the evolving nature of their relationship to Nepal. Rather than 'returning home', each trip became a step in navigating the changing landscape of their dual Nepali-Austrian heritage.

Sashi, who grew up moving between Switzerland, Burma and Nepal, also found themselves balancing virtual and in-person cultural exposure. While living abroad, they used Skype to stay connected with family in Nepal. These calls were a bridge, but their holiday visits revealed the depth of change, not just in Nepal, but in themselves. 'Each visit felt familiar yet different', Sashi reflects. The traditions and relationships they experienced virtually were redefined with each visit, helping them craft a nuanced understanding of their Nepali identity as it intersected with their global upbringing.

These stories reveal that blending virtual and in-person cultural exposure is not about recreating a static sense of home but about embracing dynamic cultural connections. While virtual communication can sustain relationships and cultural engagement, in-person visits challenge and enrich these connections, highlighting the fluidity of identity and the evolving nature of cultural belonging. For cross-cultural families, the process of weaving together these experiences is not always seamless, but it offers a pathway to understanding and supporting their children's connection to their multifaceted heritage.

Moving Past the Past

As a cross-cultural parent, I often dream of showing Marek the Nepal I grew up in. I conjure up visions of walking with him through the bustling streets of Kathmandu, lingering at the Durbar Square in Patan where I spent so many hours as a child or marveling together at the breathtaking beauty of the Khumbu region. But I know that the Nepal I carry in my heart no longer exists. The places have changed, the people have moved on, and so have I.

This realization is both bittersweet and freeing. Instead of trying to recreate my memories for Marek, I am learning to get excited about helping him form his own connections and relationships with Nepal one day. It will not be the Nepal of my childhood, and that's okay. It will be his Nepal, shaped by his experiences, his encounters and his own unique lens. My role is not to dictate what those connections should look like, but to support and facilitate his journey, equipping him with the tools and stories he needs to find his way.

In the meantime, I do what I can to bring elements of Nepal into his life. We tour special places together through shared videos, like the musical performances posted on YouTube by Nepali artists that offer glimpses of the country's evolving culture. I tell him about my memories of Boudhanath on a full moon and trekking in the Langtang region. These moments keep Nepal alive for us, a bridge between my memories and the possibilities of his future experiences.

This blending of virtual and in-person experiences is at the heart of cross-cultural parenting. It's not about perfectly replicating a past that no longer exists but about creating opportunities for our children to connect with their heritage in ways that are meaningful to them. Virtual tools provide a thread of continuity that allows us to stay current with a homeland that changes even as we watch from afar. They offer windows into evolving traditions, modern landscapes and the vibrant energy of life as it is now.

When travel becomes possible, those virtual connections lay the groundwork for a deeper, sensory immersion. They may help prepare our children to engage with a homeland that may feel unfamiliar at first, equipping them with context and curiosity to explore it for themselves. For Marek, walking through Patan's streets or gazing at the Himalayas might one day be the start of his own relationship with Nepal. I can help nurture this connection, but ultimately, he must make it his own. And perhaps, through his eyes, I might begin to build a new relationship with my once-homeland too.

Notes

(1) Stafford, 2015.
(2) Livingstone & Blum-Ross, 2020.
(3) Guttentag, 2010.
(4) Cuban, 2017; Madianou, 2016.

Takeaways from Chapter 10

Video chats make distance feel personal. Parents can use video chats to turn everyday moments, like bedtime stories or breakfast conversations, into shared experiences with family members far away.

Imaginative virtual activities bring culture home. From live storytelling sessions to guided online tours of grandparents' hometowns, parents can use media to help their children explore their heritage.

Grandparents can work with digital tools. Parents can encourage grandparents to master WhatsApp, FaceTime or other apps to open doors for passing on traditions, family jokes and memories.

Virtual gatherings capture both joy and longing. Media lets families celebrate birthdays and holidays together, while reminding everyone of the warmth they miss when they can't be in the same room.

Blending virtual meetups with in-person visits keeps bonds strong. Parents can use both video calls and in-person opportunities to deepen their children's sense of belonging, no matter where life takes them.

Reflection Questions – Chapter 10

Here are five reflection questions you might consider based on the themes included in this chapter:

(1) When it comes to passing on your cultural traditions to your children, how do you mix screen-based connections (like virtual family gatherings) with in-person visits?

(2) How have video calls, messaging apps and social media helped you stay close with friends and family who live far away? Can you share moments where it really brought you closer and any times it felt like it got in the way?

(3) Are there aspects of your cultures that feel difficult or impossible to pass on through a screen? Why?

(4) Have you or your children felt that video chats just didn't quite live up to being together in person? How, if at all, did you work through that disconnect?

(5) What creative approaches could you use to make virtual interactions with family and friends more meaningful for your children? Could incorporating storytelling, games and shared activities help?

Activity: Tales that Travel

Purpose and Benefits

This activity offers a quick and engaging way for children to bond with distant family members through creative storytelling. It provides a fun cultural connection, fosters imagination and strengthens intergenerational ties, all within a short and manageable timeframe.

Duration: 15 minutes

- Setup and introduction: 3–4 minutes.
- Story creation: 8–10 minutes.
- Wrap-up and planning: 1–2 minutes.

What You Will Need

- Video call platform (e.g. WhatsApp, Zoom, Skype).
- Paper and colored pencils or markers.

How to Do It

(1) **Set Up the Call (1–2 minutes):**
- Start a video call with a relative.
- Ensure both participants have materials like paper and colored pencils ready. You could also choose to use a multi-user creative platform like a Padlet or Google Slides as well.

(2) **Story Introduction (2 minutes):**
- Choose a simple theme, such as a family folktale or a story from your relative's childhood.

(3) **Create the Story (8–10 minutes):**
- Invite the relative or friend to draw or narrate while the child asks questions, suggests characters or adds ideas.
- Take turns creating a short narrative together. Keep it light and fun to fit within the 8–10-minute window.

(4) **Save the Work (1 minute):**
- Take a photo or screenshot of the drawing to save for future sessions.

(5) **Plan the Next Session (1 minute):**
- Decide whether to continue the story in the next call or start a new one.

Reflection or Follow-Up (Optional)

- How did the story reflect your family's cultural background or shared experiences?

- What did you enjoy most about the storytelling process?
- How could you expand this activity with new themes or more family members?

Activity: 15-Minute Journeys

Purpose and Benefits

In just 15 minutes, this activity allows children to explore their cultural heritage through short virtual tours guided by a parent or grandparent. It encourages cultural curiosity and connection while fitting easily into a busy schedule, making it a simple yet meaningful way to bond and learn.

Duration: 15 minutes

- Preparation: 2–3 minutes.
- Virtual tour: 10 minutes.
- Wrap-up: 2 minutes.

What You Will Need

- Access to a short YouTube video or virtual tour (around 10 minutes long).
- A device for watching the video (e.g. computer, tablet or phone).
- A video call platform (optional, if guiding the tour remotely).

How to Do It

(1) **Prepare the Tour (2–3 minutes):**
  - Find a short YouTube video or virtual tour with a cultural theme or personal significance, such as a walking tour of a family member's hometown or a cultural festival.

(2) **Start the Tour (10 minutes):**
  - Watch the virtual tour together on a shared screen or with a parent/relative guiding the experience.
  - Add personal insights during the tour, such as:
    - o 'This market is where we used to shop.'
    - o 'This festival is a big part of our culture.'

(3) **Wrap Up (2 minutes):**
  - Engage the child by asking quick reflection questions:
    - o 'What was your favorite part?'
    - o 'What would you like to learn about next time?'

(4) **Follow Up:**
  - Suggest what the next virtual tour might cover to maintain curiosity, such as another town, a cultural event or a historical site.

Reflection or Follow-Up (Optional)

- How did this virtual journey connect your child to their cultural heritage?
- What new stories or insights came up during the experience?
- How can you build on this activity with additional virtual tours or stories?

Part 5
Navigate the Paths Ahead

11 Accept the Journey

Figure 11.1 Cross-cultural parenting has no final destination. (credit A. Desai)

I opened this book by sharing my personal journey growing up between cultures. This is a journey that began long before I became a parent. Moving between Nepal and the Czech Republic multiple times and attending an international school shaped me, challenged me and ultimately made me who I am today. Since then, I have encountered many people who also experience some version of this cross-cultural experience. Whether by choice or circumstance, there are many people who move between countries, grow up between worlds or find they are parenting across cultural boundaries. Each of these people has their own story to tell. There are also things we have in common. We have to learn to adapt, to cross cultures and to be resilient if we choose to hold on to these connections.

I was able to have so many conversations with people who have crossed cultures as I worked on this book. I learned so much along the way about how people navigate their in-between cultural realities. What stands out to me is that we discover something new when we move to a place not fully our own emotionally, geographically and culturally.

And, ultimately, living a cross-cultural life is in itself a shared experience, regardless of where you have come from and what brought you here. I have spoken to people who chose to move. I have also spoken to people who had to move. And yes, life circumstances do change how we experience our cross-cultural realities. At the same time, some of the joys and challenges of navigating multiple identities are the same. We all live between worlds, exist between time zones and hold on to the past as much as we hope for the future.

What I've also come to realize is that my cross-cultural journey didn't begin with me. Just like it does for many families, crossing cultures extends far back into my family's history. After World War II, my grandfather was stationed in India as part of a mission to install Czechoslovak electric meters. My mother spent part of her childhood in India, attending a Soviet/Russian school. Even now, she reflects on that time with vivid detail, recalling how it shaped her perspective and left an indelible mark on her sense of identity. Her story reminds me that the influence of cross-cultural experiences can ripple across generations, leaving traces that shape who we are and how we engage with the world.

Through my mother's story, my own experiences and now raising my son, it's clear that cross-cultural parenting isn't something that has a clear beginning and end date. It's a marathon, not a sprint. From childhood, to adolescence and adulthood, each phase of life brings its own set of challenges and opportunities. Cross-cultural parenting is an ongoing process of adaptation, reflection and growth, both for parents and for children.

For the parents I met, this journey comes with additional challenges. Some face limited resources, whether financial, time-related or a lack of local cultural connections. Some had no access to community groups, family members or cultural institutions to help foster a sense of cross-cultural belonging. These constraints can make it difficult for these parents to teach their children additional languages, celebrate cultural traditions with each other and ultimately to maintain meaningful ties to heritage.

Other parents I met faced prejudice or stereotyping based on their ethnicity or assumptions about their home country. This often added another layer of complexity to their efforts to instill pride in their heritage or nurture their children's cultural identities. The lack of understanding or acceptance from their broader community can lead to diminished opportunities for connection. Parents can also feel isolated in their efforts to create a cross-cultural environment at home.

Reflecting on my family's cross-cultural journey, I see how this experience evolves over time. Each generation faces its own unique context and challenges but also discovers its own tools for maintaining cultural identity. For my mother, it was the experience of attending a Soviet school in India which led to lifelong fluency in Russian. I have the ability to access and use popular culture and media to ensure my son remains connected to his Czech, Nepali and Indian heritage while growing up in the United States.

I have learned a lot through the interviews, interactions and insights that shaped this book, and this book is so much more than a research project to me. I have had the opportunity to learn and connect with parents and communities that have so much to share. I got to listen and learn from the lived experiences and stories of cross-cultural parents and children. I have questioned my own assumptions and continued to learn from others. And I have worked to share it all with you in this book.

So, I now turn to you, dear reader, and leave you with these final takeaways.

Let Identities Evolve

To parent across cultures, we have to embrace change, not just in our children, but in us as well. Children raised between cultures experience shifting identities as they navigate the cultural landscapes they inhabit. What feels central to their identity one day might take a backseat the next, as they are influenced by their age, the environments they live in and the people who surround them. These shifts can feel disorienting for us as parents and for our children, but they are also a natural and vital part of growing up in a multicultural world.

Gabriela is a mother from Chile raising her children in the United States (who you met in several chapters). She laughed as she shared how her kids often seem more American in their everyday lives. They play baseball. They like mac and cheese. They use phrases like 'that's awesome!' Yet, when Chile takes the field during a soccer (football) match, her children become fiercely Chilean. 'It's as if they're rediscovering their roots every time', she said. For Gabriela, these moments are a reminder that cultural identity isn't fixed. Her children, like many other children, intertwine their identities and draw different strands to respond to specific situations.

This dynamic interweaving is not just normal, it's essential. Cultural identity doesn't have to be an either/or choice. It can be a celebration of both/and. A child can feel fully American AND fully Chilean, or Indian AND Czech, without needing to pick one over the other. As parents, one of the greatest gifts we can offer our children is the freedom to explore this duality (or even multiplicity) of identities without fear or judgment. By validating their children's experiences, whether it's cheering for a national team or embracing a holiday tradition, we can create a safe space where cultural exploration can thrive.

Of course, this journey doesn't happen in a vacuum. Where a family lives, the resources available and the cultural communities they engage with all shape how children experience their identities. Some families are fortunate to live in vibrant multicultural neighborhoods where their heritage is celebrated and reinforced. For example, a child growing up hearing their heritage language spoken on the streets or attending lively cultural festivals may feel an immediate connection to their cross-cultural identities.

Not every family has that luxury. Gabriela herself noted that her family celebrates Chilean holidays at home. For families without local resources (whether due to financial constraints, geographic isolation or limited access), maintaining these connections can feel like an uphill battle.

This is where creativity becomes essential. Parents can turn to media to fill the gaps, using films, music and online communities to keep cultural traditions alive. For children growing up between cultures, their identities are forged in this in-between (or third) space that blends their surroundings, connections and experiences. As parents, our goal isn't to lock our children into a single identity but to nurture their ability to adapt, explore and redefine who they are as they grow.

It's a Long-Term Commitment

Cross-cultural parenting is a lifelong commitment for everyone involved. You will evolve alongside your children as you respond to your family's circumstances and the world around you. What feels right and effective at one stage of your child's life might need to be entirely reimagined at the next.

Isabela's story (mentioned in Chapter 10) illustrates this beautifully. A Greek mother raising her children in Norway, Isabela started out determined to immerse her kids in Greek culture and language. 'When they were little, we spoke Greek at home, and they spent time every week talking with my mother', she shared. But as her children grew older, their educational needs and the family's priorities shifted. Living in a multilingual environment, Isabela and her husband decided to focus on French and Spanish through their children's school. They added Norwegian as their children prepared for their next relocation. 'Greek became less of a focus', she explained, 'but it wasn't lost. It just had to fit into the bigger picture of what they needed at that point'.

Isabela did not abandon her heritage. She just made thoughtful choices when it came to balancing her children's cultural roots with their immediate needs and future aspirations. Her story reflects a truth many parents face: cross-cultural parenting often involves compromise. We may start with a vision of raising perfectly bilingual or culturally immersed children, only to realize that life rarely follows our ideal plans. Work schedules, financial constraints or a lack of local resources can mean that not every tradition, language or connection is preserved in the way we initially imagined. When your kids are young, the focus might be on teaching a heritage language or celebrating traditional holidays. As they grow older, you might shift to exploring cultural narratives through media, focusing on skills like cooking family recipes, or simply sharing stories about their roots during quiet moments together.

Isabela's decision to adapt her family's approach to cultural education highlights another important lesson: practicality matters. Not every family has the resources to send their children to heritage language schools or participate in elaborate cultural traditions. For some, staying connected to their roots means using what's available: borrowing books from the library, watching subtitled movies or leaning on digital tools to stay in touch with faraway relatives. These choices aren't lesser; they're creative solutions to the realities of modern parenting.

In the end, cross-cultural parenting plays out over years and decades, not days and weeks, and your children's relationship with their heritage will likely look different from your own. There's no finish line to cross; instead, there are countless opportunities to adapt, reflect and try again.

Use Any Media

Access to local cultural resources may be hard to find for some cross-cultural parents. There may be no local community groups. They may not be able to find in-person language classes. Extended family may live too far away to offer any real support. This can all feel daunting. But this is where taking a *by any media* approach can really help. They can use media, in all its diverse forms, to bridge the gap and keep cultural connections alive in creative and meaningful ways.

We met Layla, an Egyptian parent raising her children in the United States, in Chapter 4. Layla uses all tools that are available to her to support her cross-cultural parenting. This includes media. She watches videos with her children to teach them how to prepare traditional dishes, celebrate festivals and even sing songs she remembers from her childhood. In Layla's home, media is an indispensable cross-cultural parenting tool.

Layla emphasizes that her use of media isn't about replacing more meaningful in-person interactions that her children have with their Egyptian relatives. It is about adapting them to her reality. 'I want my children to know where they come from, even if we can't go back often', she says. By being intentional in how she incorporates media into her family's routine, she ensures that cultural experiences remain vibrant and meaningful.

Layla's story reminds me that cultural transmission doesn't have to always be elaborate or expensive. You just need to think about what tools you have access to and how you want to use them. Parents juggle demanding work schedules, tight budgets and geographic isolation. Media can help. FaceTime calls with relatives in different countries keep them involved in your children's lives. Music streaming apps can introduce children to their parents' music. Watching a film in a parent's native language can immerse children in the sounds, language and values that shaped their parents. Whether it's cooking along with a YouTube video, exploring heritage languages through language apps or taking a dance class, media is a tool that cross-cultural parents can use.

Ultimately, the *by any media* approach is about creativity and intention. It's about finding ways to share your heritage, no matter the obstacles. Whether it's through virtual family gatherings, sharing traditional recipes via video call or simply playing around with languages over dinner, these small but intentional acts foster a sense of pride and belonging in your children.

Stay Connected

Cross-cultural children often wrestle with questions like, 'Where do I fit?' For them, keeping a link to their heritage isn't just about tradition. It can be a real source of strength.

Take Mai in the Netherlands (you met her in Chapters 5 and 9). She makes sure her daughter stays in touch with family in Vietnam through video calls. These calls aren't just about quick hellos. They're chances for the family to share stories and traditions. They also create moments for Mai's daughter to practice her Vietnamese naturally. 'It's not the same as being there', Mai says, 'but it really helps her feel connected'. Those chats become an emotional thread, connecting her daughter to something bigger than her day-to-day life.

What Mai's story shows us is true for many cross-cultural parents. Keeping family ties alive nurtures a child's sense of belonging. This can happen in-person or online. It can be a long-term commitment to language classes or occasional moments interspersed in our daily lives. Ideally, it is both.

Over time, that feeling of connection becomes a safety net. A grandparent's story shared over video chat or a favorite song sung at the dinner table can give kids the confidence to explore their identities. They will know that their roots matter but don't limit them. As parents raising kids between cultures, our job is simple yet powerful: help them feel at home in themselves, wherever they are.

It's Your Journey Too

Every family's cross-cultural journey will be different. Of course, you'll see familiar themes. They will juggle languages. They will want to honor traditions. They will want to help their children feel they belong. But the specifics and strategies that shape each family's experience will vary widely. A lot will depend on the family's circumstances. Did they migrate for work? Are they navigating life as refugees? Are they blending cultures in a cross-cultural marriage? Each family's path will also depend on other considerations like economic status, geographic location and personal background.

Marisol is an educator and a cross-cultural parent (whom you met in Chapter 8). For her, keeping her kids connected to their Costa Rican roots came down to one simple habit: reading in Spanish. 'Speaking the language isn't enough', she says. 'If you want your children to develop a rich connection to their roots, they need to read in that language'. Her approach was pragmatic: setting aside a small, consistent part of the day for heritage language reading, no matter how hectic life became. It wasn't about perfection, but about persistence.

Other families find their own ways. Some plan regular trips back 'home'. Others sign up for weekend language classes or cultural camps. And when budgets or distance get in the way, they get creative. They tune into traditional music on Spotify, or stream films to 'tour' their homelands. These workarounds keep culture alive even when the old-school approach isn't possible.

It's also a relief to let go of perfection. You won't manage to hold on to every ritual or master every holiday recipe. And that's OK. Cross-cultural parenting is about adapting, improvising and finding what sticks. Maybe you simplify Diwali celebrations or practice a few phrases of Arabic during breakfast. Those imperfect moments are what matter most.

At the end of the day, what matters isn't ticking every cultural box, but embracing the journey together. As you and your children learn from each other, you'll build a family story that's both personal and enduring. One that is uniquely your own.

Epilogue

I really didn't know what to say in this epilogue. I started working on this book in 2021, which now feels like a very long time ago. We had emerged from the lockdowns that defined the COVID-19 pandemic with a sense that the world just might open up a little more. Writing this Epilogue as 2025 draws to a close, I am filled with low-grade anxiety and a sense of dread about what the coming months and years will bring us. In all honesty, I even thought about walking away from this book. How could I focus on the joys and possibilities of cross-cultural parenting as the very existence of people whose identities cross cultures and borders seems to be coming under threat? What can this book offer? And, why should I continue to work on it?

I sat with these questions for a long time and came to this conclusion: this book makes sense because it is a testament to the lived experiences of cross-cultural parents and their children. Our stories deserve to be told. We should have the chance to listen and learn from each other. We should highlight and celebrate the real opportunities and challenges of cross-cultural parenting. We should encourage each other to stay the course. So this book is my way of pointing to the possible light at the end of the tunnel.

In fact, my own family's cross-cultural journey has not been an easy one. Between a communist government in Czechoslovakia and an autocratic monarchy in Nepal, my parents faced forced separation, travel restrictions and extreme financial difficulties as they raised me. There were so many moments when they could have 'thrown in the towel' and walked away from their cross-cultural commitments to each other and to me. I vividly recall witnessing some of those moments of crisis as a child. We struggled with money. We struggled with prejudice. We struggled with immigration issues. But my parents persisted. And my life has been so much more full and richer because they did. I am comfortable with who I am and where I have come from. I am also open to where life may lead me. I claim and celebrate my cross-cultural life.

As a parent, I now want to give this same opportunity to my son. I want him to feel that his cross-cultural identity is a gift and an opportunity. He can choose to tap into who he is in any way he wants, but he should be aware that he is, as another cross-cultural child put it, 'more than the sum of his parts'. I can think of no better way to do this than by learning from and with others who are on a similar journey. And in the end, this is what this book is all about. It is an invitation for us to listen and learn from each other.

So I do not claim to have all the answers. I will also be the first to acknowledge that there is much more to consider when it comes to cross-cultural parenting. I focused on children under 12. I also highlight collaborative uses of media, recognizing that this is a limited-use scenario. I hope that others will pick up where this book leaves off when it comes to debates surrounding media and look forward to continuing the conversation.

There may really be dark times ahead. The sun may eventually break through. I have no idea what the next months and years will bring for those of us living in between cultures. But, I do know that I feel much stronger knowing that I am not alone on my cross-cultural parenting journey. There are other parents on this journey too. Some of them are included in this book. Others I have yet to meet. So my hope is that this book helps us connect and find each other, making us stronger and more resilient no matter what may come next.

Sangita Shresthova

References

Alexander, J.J. and Sandahl, I.D. (2016) *The Danish Way of Parenting: What the Happiest People in the World Know About Raising Confident, Capable Kids*. TarcherPerigee.

Anderson, B. (1983) *Imagined Communities: Reflections on the Origin and Spread of Nationalism*. Verso.

Annamalai, E. (2010) Politics of language in India. In P.R. Brass (ed.) *Routledge Handbook on South Asian Politics* (pp. 323–349). Routledge.

Appadurai, A. (1988) How to make a national cuisine: Cookbooks in contemporary India. *Comparative Studies in Society and History* 30 (1), 3–24. http://www.jstor.org/stable/179020.

Appadurai, A. (1996) *Modernity at Large*. University of Minnesota Press.

Baker, C. (2007) *A Parents' and Teachers' Guide to Bilingualism* (3rd edn). Multilingual Matters.

Bales, C.E. (2022) *Invisible Outsider: From Battling Bullies to Building Bridges, My Life as a Third Culture Kid*. Self-Published.

Barry, B. (2001) *Culture and Equality: An Egalitarian Critique of Multiculturalism*. Harvard University Press.

Benet-Martínez, V. and Haritatos, J. (2005) Bicultural identity integration (BII): Components and psychosocial antecedents. *Journal of Personality* 73 (4), 1015–1049.

Berry, J.W. (1997) Immigration, acculturation, and adaptation. *Applied Psychology: An International Review* 46 (1), 5–34. https://doi.org/10.1111/j.1464-0597.1997.tb01087.x.

Bhabha, H.K. (1994) *The Location of Culture*. Routledge.

Bornstein, M.H., Putnick, D.L. and Lansford, J.E. (2011) Parenting attributions and attitudes in cross-cultural perspective. *Parenting: Science and Practice* 11 (2-3), 214–237. https://doi.org/10.1080/15295192.2011.585568. PMID: 21927591; PMCID: PMC3173779.

Cardinal, L. (2004) The limits of bilingualism in Canada. *Nationalism and Ethnic Politics* 10 (1), 79–103. https://doi.org/10.1080/13537110490450782.

Catalano, T. (2016) *Talking About Global Migration: Implications for Language Teaching*. Multilingual Matters.

Civitello, L. (2011) *Cuisine and Culture: A History of Food and People* (3rd edn). John Wiley & Sons.

Counihan, C., Van Esterik, P. and Julier, A. (2017) *Food and Culture: A Reader* (3rd edn). Routledge.

Craft, A.L., Rowley, C.A. and Perry-Jenkins, M. (2022) Multiracial families: Differences in values & relational outcomes. *Journal of Child and Family Studies* 31 (3), 629–648. https://doi.org/10.1007/s10826-022-02247-8.

Crawford, J. (2004) *Educating English Learners: Language Diversity in the Classroom*. Bilingual Education Services.

Crenshaw, K. (1991) Mapping the margins: Intersectionality, identity politics, and violence against women of color. *Stanford Law Review* 43 (6), 1241–1299.

Crowther, G. (2013) *Eating Culture: An Anthropological Guide to Food*. University of Toronto Press.

Cuban, S. (2017) *Transnational Family Communication: Immigrants and ICTs*. Palgrave Macmillan.

Davis, K. (2023) *Technology's Child: Digital Media's Role in the Ages and Stages of Growing Up*. MIT Press.

De Houwer, A. (2009) *Bilingual First Language Acquisition*. Multilingual Matters. https:// doi.org/10.21832/9781847691507.

Druckerman, P. (2012) *Bringing Up Bébé: One American Mother Discovers the Wisdom of French Parenting*. Penguin Press.

Earl, J. (2018) Episode 18: Jennifer Earl, internet activism and fake news. Half hour of heterodoxy [Podcast]. *Heterodox Academy*.

Gándara, P. and Hopkins, M. (2010) *Forbidden Language: English Learners and Restrictive Language Policies*. Teachers College Press.

García, O. and Li, W. (2014) *Translanguaging: Language, Bilingualism and Education*. Palgrave Macmillan.

Gardner, M.R. (2018) *Worlds Apart: A Third Culture Kid's Journey*. Doorlight Publications.

Gautam, B.L. (2021) Language politics in Nepal: A socio-historical overview. *Journal of World Languages* 7 (2), 355–374. https://doi.org/10.1515/jwl-2021-0010.

Geiger, A.W. and Livingston, G. (2019) *8 Facts about Love and Marriage in America*. Pew Research Center.

Georgas, J., Berry, J.W., van de Vijver, F.J.R., Kağitçibaşi, Ç. and Poortinga, Y.H. (eds) (2006) *Families Across Cultures: A 30-Nation Psychological Study*. Cambridge University Press.

Gold, J. (2024) Parents are ditching screen time limits for kids against expert advice. *Los Angeles Times*, 26 June.

Gordon, M. (1964) *Assimilation in American Life: The Role of Race, Religion, and National Origins*. Oxford University Press.

Granovetter, M.S. (1973) The strength of weak ties. *American Journal of Sociology* 78 (6), 1360–1380. http://www.jstor.org/stable/2776392.

Grin, F. (2003) *Language Policy Evaluation and the European Charter for Regional or Minority Languages*. Palgrave Macmillan.

Grosjean, F. (2010) *Bilingual: Life and Reality*. Harvard University Press.

Guernsey, L. (2012) *Screen Time: How Electronic Media – from Baby Videos to Educational Software – Affects Your Young Child*. Basic Books.

Gutmann, A. (ed.) (1994) *Multiculturalism: Examining the Politics of Recognition*. Princeton University Press.

Guttentag, D.A. (2010) Virtual reality: Applications and implications for tourism. *Tourism Management* 31 (5), 637–651. https://doi.org/10.1016/j.tourman.2009.07.003.

Haidt, J. (2024) *The Anxious Generation: How the Great Rewiring of Childhood Is Causing an Epidemic of Mental Illness*. Penguin Press.

Halford, W.K. and van de Vijver, F. (2020) *Cross-Cultural Family Research and Practice*. Academic Press.

Hall, J.A. (2017) Humor in romantic relationships: A meta-analysis. *Journal of the International Association for Relationship Research* 24 (2), 306–322.

Hall, S. (1997) *Representation: Cultural Representations and Signifying Practices*. Sage.

Hills, M. (2002) *Fan Cultures*. Routledge.

International Organization for Migration (2020) *World Migration Report 2020*. International Organization for Migration.

Jenkins, H. (1992) *Textual Poachers: Television Fans and Participatory Culture*. Routledge.

Jenkins, H. (2006) *Convergence Culture: Where Old and New Media Collide*. NYU Press.

Jenkins, H., Ford, S. and Green, J. (2013) *Spreadable Media: Creating Value and Meaning in a Networked Culture*. NYU Press.

Jenkins, H., Shresthova, S., Gamber-Thompson, L., Kligler-Vilenchik, R. and Zimmerman, A. (2016) *By Any Media Necessary: The New Youth Activism*. NYU Press.

Jones, G.W. (2012) International marriage in Asia: What do we know, and what do we need to know? *Asia Research Institute Working Paper Series* No. 174, 2–3.

Kamenetz, A. (2018) *The Art of Screen Time: How Your Family Can Balance Digital Media and Real Life*. PublicAffairs.

Kao, K.T. and Do Rozario, R.A. (2008) Imagined spaces: The implications of song and dance for Bollywood's diasporic communities. *Continuum* 22 (3), 313–326. https://doi.org/10.1080/10304310802001755.

Kim, K. (2017) Cross-border marriages in south korea and the challenges of rising multiculturalism. *International Migration* 55 (3), 71–88.

Kresnicka, S. (2020) Screen time: Beyond the hardware. *Pop Junctions Blog: Reflections On Entertainment, Pop Culture, Activism, Media Literacy, Fandom and More.* https://henryjenkins.org/blog/2020/8/30/rethinking-screen-time-in-the-age-of-covid-19-part-three.

Kymlicka, W. (2000) *Multicultural Citizenship: A Liberal Theory of Minority Rights.* Oxford University Press.

Kymlicka, W. (2009) *Multicultural Odysseys: Navigating the New International Politics of Diversity.* Oxford University Press.

Lanzieri, G. (2012) Merging populations: A look at marriages with foreign-born persons in European countries. *Eurostat* 29, 1–4.

Lenard, P.T. (2016) *Trust, Democracy, and Multicultural Challenges.* Penn State University Press.

Livingstone, S. and Blum-Ross, A. (2020) *Parenting for a Digital Future: How Hopes and Fears about Technology Shape Children's Lives.* Oxford University Press.

Madianou, M. (2017) 'Doing family' at a distance: Transnational family practices in polymedia environments. In L. Hjorth, H. Horst, A. Galloway and G. Bell (eds) *The Routledge Companion to Digital Ethnography* (pp. 102–111). Routledge.

Morris, A.J. and Lansford, J.E. (2022) Parenting from a cultural and global perspective. In A. Morris and J. Lansford (eds) *The Cambridge Handbook of Parenting: Volume 2: Social and Emotional Aspects of Parenting* (pp. 389–408). Cambridge University Press.

Nayani, F. (2020) *Raising Multiracial Children: Tools for Nurturing Identity in a Racially Divided World.* North Atlantic Books.

Oldenburg, R. (1999) *The Great Good Place: Cafes, Coffee Shops, Bookstores, Bars, Hair Salons, and Other Hangouts at the Heart of a Community.* Marlowe & Company.

Phinney, J.S. (1990) Ethnic identity in adolescents and adults: Review of research. *Psychological Bulletin* 108 (3), 499–514.

Pollock, D.C. and Van Reken, R.E. (2009) *Third Culture Kids: Growing Up Among Worlds* (rev. edn). Nicholas Brealey Publishing.

Raja, R., Ma, J., Tao, R., Ullah, S., Li, X.Y., Shafi, M.M. (2024) Social identity development in transnational marriages of international students in China. *Humanities and Social Sciences Communications* 11, 203. https://doi.org/10.1057/s41599-023-02396-1.

Ray, K. and Tulasi, S. (eds) (2012) *Curried Cultures: Food, Globalization and South Asia.* University of California Press.

Reitz, J., Dion, K., Phan, M., Breton, R., Dion, K. and Banerjee, R. (2009) *Multiculturalism and Social Cohesion, Potentials and Challenges of Diversity.* Springer.

Rico, B., Jacobs, P. and Coritz, A. (2023) Census shows increase in multiracial population in all age categories. *United States Census Bureau*, 1 June.

Rideout, V. and Robb, M.B. (2020) *The Common Sense Census: Media Use by Kids Age Zero to Eight, 2020.* Common Sense Media.

Romano, D. (2008) *Intercultural Marriage: Promises and Pitfalls.* Nicholas Brealey.

Said, E.W. (1978) *Orientalism.* Pantheon Books.

Selin, H. (ed.) (2013) *Parenting Across Cultures: Childrearing, Motherhood and Fatherhood in Non-Western Cultures.* Springer.

Shresthova, S. (2011) *Is It All About Hips?: Around the World with Bollywood Dance.* Sage Publications.

Stafford, L. (2015) Long-distance relationships. In C.R. Berger, M.E. Roloff, S.R. Wilson, J.P. Dillard, J. Caughlin and D. Solomon (eds) *The International Encyclopedia of Interpersonal Communication* (pp. 1–3). Wiley Blackwell.

Trask, B.S. (2010) *Globalization and Families: Accelerated Systemic Social Change*. Springer.

Turkle, S. (2012) *Alone Together: Why We Expect More from Technology and Less from Each Other*. Basic Books.

Twenge, J.M. (2017) *iGen: Why Today's Super-Connected Kids Are Growing Up Less Rebellious, More Tolerant, Less Happy – and Completely Unprepared for Adulthood*. Atria Books.

Useem, R.H. and Downie, R.D. (1976) Third-culture kids. *Today's Education* 65 (3), 103–105.

Ward, R. and Singh, A. (2015) The *Great British Bake Off* 2015: The final – Nadiya crowned winner. *The Telegraph*, 8 October.

Weber, E. (1976) *Peasants into Frenchmen: The Modernization of Rural France, 1870–1914*. Stanford University Press.

Wenger, E. (1998) *Communities of Practice: Learning, Meaning, and Identity*. Cambridge University Press.

Williams, C. (2000) Bilingual teaching and language distribution at 16+. *International Journal of Bilingual Education and Bilingualism* 3 (2), 129–148.

Williams, R. (1958) *Culture and Society, 1780–1950*. Chatto & Windus.

Index

For Product Safety Concerns and Information please contact our EU Authorised
Representative:

Easy Access System Europe

Mustamäe tee 50

10621 Tallinn

Estonia

gpsr.requests@easproject.com

www.ingramcontent.com/pod-product-compliance
Lightning Source LLC
Chambersburg PA
CBHW072249270326
41930CB00010B/2325